PARENTING TEENS
WITH LOVE AND LOGIC

PARENTING TEENS WITH LOVE & LOGIC

Preparing Adolescents for Responsible Adulthood

Foster W. Cline, M.D.
and Jim Fay

P.O. Box 35007, Colorado Springs, Colorado 80935

Library of Congress Catalog Card Number:
    92-64090
ISBN 08910-96957

Cover photograph: Comstock, Inc.

The actual text of *Parenting Teens with Love and Logic*
was written by Tom Morton.

Some of the anecdotal illustrations in this book are true
to life and are included with the permission of the persons
involved. All other illustrations are composites of real
situations, and any resemblance to people living or dead
is coincidental.

Printed in the United States of America

6 7 8 9 10 11 12 13 14 15 16 17 18 19 20/99 98 97 96 95

CONTENTS

PART THREE: LOVE-AND-LOGIC PARENTING PEARLS

To my wife, Shirley,
whose love, support, and wisdom
have always been a source
of motivation and strength.
— Jim Fay

To all the parents
and children
who were my teachers
and to my wife
who gave support.
— Foster W. Cline

INTRODUCTION

Parents whose children are now turning twelve and thirteen know their kids face far greater challenges than they did just a few short years ago.

That means that *parents* are facing far greater challenges than they did just a few short years ago.

But most parents learn parenting simply by doing it. They feel joy and relief when their children learn how to live and grow on their own. They feel the sting of disappointment when an approach fails. They suffer the dread of failure when it looks like their children — despite their best efforts — somehow aren't going to "turn out right."

This kind of trial-and-error experience can be pretty nerve-wracking in light of the consequences looming over our kids' lives.

Do you find yourself wondering whether you're doing the right things to equip your kids for the challenges they're facing? Do you wonder how to equip *yourself* for the challenges you're facing?

Take heart. You're not alone. Parenting is a challenge—and an opportunity—for anyone with teenagers. It doesn't matter what kind of batting average they've been maintaining. Adolescence can be a whole new ball game.

We (Foster and Jim) have watched our own children grow through adolescence. And we have dealt with thousands of other parents and teens through our respective professions of psychiatry and education. We have some coaching tips we're convinced will help you.

THE LOVE-AND-LOGIC APPROACH

We offer an approach called "parenting with love and logic." We spelled it out in an earlier book by that name. You may have read it, learned its principles, and applied them to your children.

If you haven't read *Parenting with Love and Logic,* you might find it helpful to get hold of a copy, especially to read the first part, although we will cover many of those same principles from a different perspective in this book. If you have read the first book, you've got a good jump on the material here. When you come to sections you're familiar with, read them as a refresher course in love-and-logic parenting—or simply skim through them.

Why do we call our approach "love-and-logic parenting"? The first half, "love," is essential to parenting. As you will learn, however, "love" does not mean hovering around your teens to protect them from all the rocks flung at them by the world. Neither does "love" mean tolerating outlandish, disrespectful, or illegal behavior. Rather, *love means empowering teens to make their own decisions, to live with their own mistakes, and to grow through the consequences.*

The second half of our approach, "logic," centers on the consequences themselves. Most decisions and mistakes lead to logical consequences. And those consequences, when accompanied by empathy — compassion for the disappointment, frustration, and pain that teens experience — will drive home lessons powerfully enough to change a teen's thinking for a lifetime.

Love-and-logic doesn't mean that we transfer all of our answers or values to our teens. Instead, we help place them in situations where they can discover answers and values on their own.

HOW THIS BOOK IS ORGANIZED

This book is written in three sections. Part 1 adapts concepts from the first *Parenting with Love and Logic* book specifically to teenagers. We discuss effective and ineffective parenting styles. We also explain how teens deal with self-esteem, control, decisions, and consequences, and how parents meet the consequences of their teens' decisions with empathy. These concepts lay the foundation for effective parenting of teens.

In part 2, we explore development in teens: how children grow from childhood into adolescence (and how parents go through growth phases with them!), and how they react to internal as well as external change. We conclude this section with practical guidelines and encouragement for parents on how to raise responsible teenagers.

In the third part we get down to nuts-and-bolts specifics. We offer thirty-three love-and-logic "pearls" dealing with everyday problems and issues most parents will face during their children's teenage years. Although these strategy nuggets are short and to the point, they should be read only after the principles in the first two parts of the book have been studied and understood.

We believe that love-and-logic parenting works, or we

wouldn't have written this book. But no parenting system works perfectly every time. Actually, love-and-logic parenting is not so much a *system* as an *attitude*. When it's applied in the context of a healthy relationship with our teens, this attitude will free our teens to grow in maturity as they grow in years. It will teach them to think, to decide, and to live with their decisions. They will learn responsibility as we learn to live with less control and make peace with our own abilities and shortcomings. As our children grow older and wiser, we'll gain not just a more mature child, but a friend as well.

Not all teens are alike, of course. Children who seemed so similar when they were younger than age eleven develop in much different ways in their teenage years. No book on teenagers can anticipate every physical change or every outside influence.

Therefore, in this book we assume that although teens share basic similarities, each family has its own kind of child. One teen's rebellion is another teen's independence. The closeness and quality of the parent-child relationship will vary from one family to another. And some kids are just plain different. So don't be alarmed if you don't see your teen grinning from behind every page.

Another assumption we're making is that the principles in this book will not be abused. A how-to book, especially one that offers advice on a matter as sensitive as parenting teenagers, can often be misused. For example, just because we believe that teens should live with the consequences of their decisions in no way implies that parents should look the other way if their children are involved in life-threatening acts such as playing with loaded weapons.

We also assume that parents who read this book are caring and loving people. Abusive parents could use these principles and possibly cause harm to their teen. Unfortunately, most parents who are abusive don't recognize or acknowledge it. Parents who suspect that they may be abusive should seek professional advice.

We believe parents face no greater challenge—and have no greater opportunity—than to guide their children through the teen years so they grow to enjoy productive, happy, and responsible adult lives. We believe that this book will help parents meet that challenge and rejoice in that opportunity. It's never too late to start parenting the love-and-logic way.

PART I

❖

Love-and-Logic Parents Grow Up

1
TEENAGERS 101:
Welcome to Parenting Graduate School

❖

June and Al Frank surveyed the dinner table. The silver, china, lighted tapers, and platters were decked out to a turn. They nodded to their guests — colleagues from Al's law firm — and all sat down to what promised to be a perfect evening of home entertaining.

Al and June could count on a quiet evening: their teenage son Robert was out on a date. Despite their outward ease with their guests, though, these parents harbored anxiety about their increasingly wayward son.

That anxiety wound into a knot when the phone rang during dessert. June answered the phone and called for Al with a trembling voice. Robert and Desiree were being held at the sheriff's office. They had both been drinking, so Robert — in a gesture of chivalrous cowardice — let Desiree drive. She drove the car over a curb, conveniently across the street from the police station, and shredded a tire. Both got tickets. The officer wanted to know when Al and June could come by to bail them out.

June's worst fears were realized: Her eighteen-year-old had formally embarked on a life of crime. Her face pale, she groped her way back to the table. When her guests asked what was wrong, she responded with a flat, this-happens-all-the-time voice, "Oh, the sheriff's department called and said they were detaining Robert."

Al, still on the phone, decided then and there to change his parenting style. He and June had recently attended a seminar on parenting and realized that they needed to do some things differently. Instead of coming to Robert's rescue or getting nasty as they used to do, Al decided to let Robert learn some responsibility and grow up.

"We're not coming down to the station to pick up Robert," he told the officer.

"Well, Mr. Frank, if you don't pick him up, I'll have to lock him up."

"Well, officer, whatever it takes."

Al, sporting a nervous grin, returned to the dining room just as June was clearing the table. She was fumbling for a polite way to end the evening, escort her guests to the door, and then drive to the station to bail out Robert. Al walked in, tossed a pack of cards on the table and said, "Let's play hearts." He pulled the stunned June aside, smiled, and said, "Let's not spoil a nice evening."

WHO'S IN CHARGE HERE?

For years, Robert had appeared headed for a life of irresponsibility. He lived like a slob and had increasingly resisted his parents' badgering about his sloppy appearance, grungy clothes, messy room, and that infernal music thudding through the walls.

At thirteen, Robert simply "forgot" to do his chores. The older he grew, the more defiant he became. At seventeen, he started drinking even on school nights and experimenting with drugs, both of which were murder on his grades. He went out with girls running with the wrong crowd, such as Desiree, telling his dad, "She comes from a broken home and needs a counselor," prompting Al to counter sarcastically, "Just what kind of counseling techniques are you using?"

Robert had long since blown off the hallowed family tradition of kissing his parents good night. Now they were lucky if he just yelled through the master bedroom door, "I'm home."

Al responded to Robert's moral slide by losing his temper and yelling. "You smell like a fermentation vat!" he would greet his son after a night out. Or, "You have the social traits of a bum!"

June would mutter aloud, "I know this is a kid I wouldn't take off the shelf myself."

Robert, of course, just sneered. He had his parents emotionally eating out of his hand, and he knew it.

They knew it, too. But they felt helpless to reassert control.

Then Al and June attended a seminar that introduced them to an approach called "love-and-logic parenting." They learned that parents should take care of themselves first, let their children own their own problems, and allow them to live with the consequences of their decisions.

A CHANGE OF TACTICS

After the guests from Al's law firm had gone home, later that night Al and June had another opportunity to apply those principles. At 11:00 p.m., while they were lying awake wondering if they had done the right thing, the phone rang.

"Yes, who is it?" Al answered.

"Dad," came Robert's urgent voice over the phone. "Dad, it's pretty bad down here."

"Hey, pal, is it really that bad?" Al went on the offensive. "Let's agree that if *I* get thrown into the hoosegow, *you* won't rescue *me*."

That was too much for the rattled Robert. "Okay, be that way!" he shouted, and slammed down the phone.

The phone rang fifteen minutes later. This time June answered.

"Mrs. Frank? This is Julie. I'm a counselor at the detention center. Mrs. Frank, I'm so proud of you and your husband. Robert is just fine. You'd be surprised at how many parents come down here and bail their kids out. Parents like you deserve a medal."

Al and June held off the next day as well, but Desiree's mother bailed out the two teens. June was dreading the coming confrontation. Robert, however, didn't come home right away. He delayed his return in fear of his parents' anger.

When Robert did arrive home, he was surprised to find that his parents weren't mad at him. His arrest was *his* responsibility, they communicated. They weren't going to berate him, but they weren't going to rescue him either.

This response defused any anger or defensiveness on Robert's part. Now that he knew the situation was his responsibility, he was open to doing something about it.

Robert told his parents that he would need to earn money to reimburse Desiree's mom for bail, to get the car out of impound, to tow it to a garage, and to have a new tire put on. "This is the most expensive date I've ever been on," he exclaimed.

June was amazed at Robert. "After that experience, we never used the rant-and-rave method again with the kids," she commented.

Today, Robert is a twenty-six-year-old graduate student worrying how to get grants, a social worker trying to make the world a better place, and a "picture of social responsibility," according to Al.

June now says, "It's easy for us to forget that adolescence is a phase for the teen and for us, too. But if you use the right techniques, it shortens the bad phases."

THE TIMES THEY ARE A'CHANGING

June and Al had gotten a graduate-level education in parenting. Their previous "schooling" hadn't prepared them for the intensity of the joys, sorrows, and dilemmas they faced daily and sometimes hourly with a teenager—from relationships, to acne, to jobs, to fashion, to loud music, to broken hearts, to broken laws.

Parents of teenagers invariably find out—if they haven't found out already—what Al and June learned: *children change.* And what a change!

Just a few years ago, we were changing diapers, reinforcing basic manners, ferrying kids here and there, assisting with homework, watching them play.

Sure, we lost our temper at times—or sometimes even felt like we were losing our mind. And yes, there were the inevitable and seemingly endless challenges to our parental authority. But even through the hard lessons, we were still the parent. Our child was still within our control.

But then along came a phase change that sent us scrambling back for more education: a graduate course in "Teenagers."

All of a sudden, our kids didn't look the same anymore. Tommy used to be satisfied with double-knee jeans and a T-shirt. Sally used to let Mom buy her clothes. Now Tom Junior wears jeans with no knees and Sally has a close personal relationship with every clothing clerk at the mall. Sometimes, they dress like every day is Halloween. These kids are going through bodily transformations that you think no doctor's ever heard of. Tom Junior towers above

Dad and can lift Mom off the floor with one hand. Sally is wearing Mom's clothes.

Fact is, children go through more physical changes in five years of adolescence than at any other time during their lives:

♦ Their brains change so they can think abstractly. They don't believe in Santa Claus anymore, and they're not too sure they believe in you, either.
♦ Their bodies produce more oil, making their faces break out and sending them into emotional tailspins over zits.
♦ And, in case you forgot, they become fertile.

The changes aren't just physical, either. Body development has remained constant from generation to generation, but societal influences are bombarding families and teens at warp speed, with incredible and sometimes catastrophic effects.

These social upheavals have scattered families in their wake — chief among them the "traditional" family of a working father, homemaking mother, and 2.2 children. This is old news to most of us. But what we really have trouble comprehending is the extent of the revolution in teen life. Consider:

♦ Suicide is a leading cause of death among teenagers.
♦ At least one in five children loses his or her virginity *before age thirteen.*
♦ Approximately 450,000 teenagers are arrested annually for driving under the influence of alcohol.
♦ An overwhelming percentage of teens lie regularly; they also have a lower standard of ethics than their parents.
♦ More than a fourth of high school students will drop out; 40 percent of black students will drop

out; and more than 50 percent of Hispanic students will drop out.[1]

♦ The percentage of children living with their birth parents continues to decline as the divorce rate hovers at 50 percent for all marriages.

♦ Unless major economic change occurs, this generation of teenagers will be the first to have a lower standard of living than their parents.

But family and societal changes are just the outside view. Complicating matters tremendously are the changes on the inside—what teens experience as they live through their own personal development.

BRAVING THE BRAVE NEW WORLD

As you watch your children enter the brave new world of adolescence, you can feel the sting of their volatile emotional reactions to this inner upheaval.

Being a teenager is an out-of-body experience—out of a child's body and into an adult's, or somewhere in between. Teenagers may look like an adult while acting like a two-year-old, as determined to establish their own identity as a defiant toddler. Naturally, we're concerned. Are they ready to handle the real world that waits beyond the safety of our protective care? And just as naturally, our teens grow more self-involved, questioning, and peer-oriented. They assimilate into a subculture, adopting distinctive dress and hairstyles along with music and language that often offends adult ears.

All this is grounded in a deep personal struggle with identity and self-worth. "Who am I?" is more than a throwaway line from television shows and juvenile rock songs. *It is the central question in teens' transition from dependence to independence.*

But they can seem like aliens compared to the children

we used to know! We wonder if other parents could possibly have as many sleepless nights worrying about their teenagers. Some of us wonder if our children and our marriages will survive.

Faced with this loss of control, we wonder, "What's wrong with me? Did my folks feel the same way about me when I was a teenager?"

What *did* your folks do? After all, it wasn't so long ago that *you* were cruising Main Street, singing along with Steppenwolf, tasting your first cigarettes and beer, skipping church, breaking curfew, and even getting grounded on occasion. Did your folks wonder if you would ever grow up and become a responsible adult? Yup, they did! But you made it.

Now fast-forward several frames. *You* are the parent of teenagers, and you hope in the few years left before they fly the coop that somehow they'll learn how to make decisions in the real world.

The "real world" — now there's a phrase to make us shudder. The pressures and influences everywhere today were practically unheard of in our parents' day. We're tempted to sink into despair as we watch our children face life-and-death decisions long before they're on their own. Drugs, alcohol, premarital sex, and especially suicide confront teens and even much younger children on a frequent basis. These pressures can overload parents as much as teens, perhaps even more so, especially if they're trying to parent just like their parents did a generation ago.

For example, when my (Jim's) parents said "jump," I thought they could actually make me do it. Teens today know that parents simply don't have that "my-word-is-the-law-in-this-house" control because of the social, cultural, and technological revolutions since World War II. They know they have a right to be treated with respect and dignity, not autocratic control.

Now teens say to themselves, "I'm not sure my parents

are right in what they're asking me to do and how they're asking me to do it. And my friends are saying that I don't have to put up with that." No wonder parents are stressed finding ways to work with their teenagers. And teens are stressed trying to figure out how to live with their parents. We're all braving the brave new world.

A REASON FOR HOPE

Is there any hope? We believe the answer is a resounding "Yes."

We all hope that we can raise our children in such a way that by the time they turn eighteen we can be friends, right? We look forward to meeting them on common ground as adults. But what does this mean?

Well, we know what we expect from our adult friends. We assume they will talk and act responsibly, think clearly, play with us when we want to have fun, be serious for the tough times of life, and leave us alone when we need privacy.

Why can't we expect the same from our teens?

You're probably thinking, *You must be talking about somebody else's teens. Mine just walked in at 4 a.m. They won't even be coherent until tomorrow afternoon. The only reason they would pay attention to my expectations is to figure out how to frustrate them.*

But we *are* talking about your teens. The principles we lay out in this book are relevant across the board—from shrinking violets to rebels without a cause. We're going to teach you how to apply them in the task of helping your teens become responsible adults.

Parenting requires not only commitment and hard work but also the right skills. The love-and-logic techniques are particularly well suited to teens because they emphasize good communication and a consultant approach. These fit well with the emerging independence of the typical teen.

And best of all, love-and-logic parents are building friendships with their children that should last a lifetime.

"Love-and-logic" is a win-win philosophy. Presuming genetics and social situations are stable, parents win because they love in a healthy way and establish effective control over their teens. They don't need to resort to the anger and threats that will haunt teens along the path to adulthood. Teens win because they learn responsibility and the logic of life by solving their own problems. They acquire the necessary tools for coping with the real world.

We offer this philosophy because although teens' fundamental needs are the same as they have been in past generations and across cultures, the influences and pressures on them are radically different.

Today's challenges require a new approach to parenting teens — the love-and-logic way.

NOTE
1. James Patterson and Peter Kim, *The Day America Told the Truth: What People Really Believe About Everything that Really Matters* (New York: Prentice Hall, 1991).

2

LOVE-AND-LOGIC PARENTING:
Will It Work with Teenagers?

❖

R emember how eager we were to see our children walk for the first time? We hovered over them armed with cameras, hoping to record baby's first step for all time.

Then once they were off, they were off and running—full-tilt. They ran around the kitchen, shaving it close around corners. They ran around the house, always veering toward the head of the stairs. They ran across the yard and down the block, with grown-ups in hot pursuit.

We were proud, if not a little terrified, to see how quickly they became mobile and demanded to go their own way.

Now they're teenagers. Have they finally slowed down? Just long enough to ask us for driver's education lessons and the keys to the family car. They're off and running once again—as they shift the car into reverse and head down the driveway. But they're not just driving out of the garage. They're about to drive out of our lives. As they disappear with a puff of exhaust blowing back our way, we hope they have the smarts and responsibility to make it on their own.

How should parents use these last few years to prepare their teens for leaving home? How do we prepare them to live as independent adults?

No parenting strategy is foolproof. However, we believe that wise application of love-and-logic principles will increase the odds of raising responsible teenagers who will leave home competent to face life on their own.

But before we present an overview of the love-and-logic way, first let's look at two familiar parenting styles that almost guarantee gray hair—or no hair at all—before teens drive away that last time.

HELICOPTER PARENTS

I (Jim) love helicopters because they make a lot of wind, noise, and vibration, and they don't go very fast. Their place in the world is to hover, rescue, and protect. Emergency response teams couldn't function without them.

But what if the helicopter hovers overhead when there's no emergency? Then it's a problem.

When parents insist on hovering overhead to provide constant protection, it's a nuisance. It can even hinder normal life. We call this pattern "helicopter parents." They stay close by in order to rescue their children whenever a problem arises.

To get a close look at helicopter parents, just visit your local elementary, middle, or high school. You'll see them hovering in and out the front door carrying sack lunches, field trip permission slips, homework assignments, violins, and coats. Helicopter parents watch for their beloved off-spring to send up a signal flare, and then they swoop in to shield their children from teachers, playmates, and other apparently hostile elements. You'll hear the principal muttering under his breath, "Wow! How long did it take the kid to train his parents to do stuff like that?"

Other moms and dads sometimes regard helicopter parents as model parents. After all, look at how involved they are. They seem so caring. They're always "there." Besides, the dangers are real, so kids *need* rescuing, right?

But if you look just under the surface, you'll discover that helicopter parents often do things for their kids because of the way *they*—the parents—feel. Out of "love," they will refrain from imposing consequences. Because *they* feel uncomfortable with consequences. When their children hurt, they bail them out. Because *they* hurt too.

Helicopter parents behave the way they do because they confuse *love, protection,* and *caring.* Each of these concepts is good, but they aren't synonymous with each other.

Helicopter parents won't allow their children to fail. If their kids fail, they mistakenly reason, it means they are uncaring and unloving parents. Rescuing parents often rescue out of their own needs. They unconsciously enjoy healing another's hurts. They are parents who *need to be needed,* not parents who *want to be wanted.*

Children who are raised with the "love" of helicopter parents will turn into helicopters themselves. But some day they will run out of fuel and crash in their personal lives. Why? Because *their learning opportunities were stolen from them* in the name of love.

So these kids keep breaking the speed limit because they know Dad will pay the fine, or they engage in promiscuous sex because Mom will get the birth control pills. A few years later, they flunk out of college, mishandle what little money they have, or meander about "getting their heads together." The real world, these young adults discover, doesn't offer a grand helicopter parent in the sky to heal their diseases, pay for their bounced checks, save them from irresponsible people, or literally bail them out of jail.

DRILL SERGEANT PARENTS

I (Jim) love drill sergeants because, like helicopters, they make a lot of noise and they stir things up. They're forthright and definite: "Do it or else you're grounded!" they bark.

If I were a drill sergeant and I had to take you to war with me, there might be a time when I'd have to say to you, "We're going up the hill after that machine gun nest!" The last thing I need to hear from you is, "But wait a minute, sarge! People have been hurt in situations like this. We all want to take a vote."

Drill sergeants have a place in our world, too. We couldn't go to war without them. But their style doesn't do much for parenting.

If you're not at war, raising teens by barking orders at them isn't really effective. In fact, it can cause war. We know this because many of us grew up with drill sergeants. And, by the way, that probably was the best way for a parent to handle things back then, because the whole culture believed that children must submit without protest to their parents. In those days the child was expected to grow up obediently, become an organization man, and follow orders in adulthood. He was expected to fit in.

That was okay for back then. A person could expect to have one job for life. The world was less complex, and roles were well defined. As a child, I (Jim) never criticized my dad for saying to me, "I don't care how you feel about it: you get it done *now*!" When I grew up, I vowed never to be like him. But I became more like him than I could ever have imagined!

It's a hard habit to break. Drill sergeant parents feel that the more they bark control, the better their children will be in the long run. These parents are on a power trip. They assume, "These kids will be disciplined; they'll know how to act right."

Although the drill sergeant style seems so much different from the helicopter style, the results are the same. Children of drill sergeant parents don't know how to make decisions. They've been ordered around all their lives, listening to voices coming from outside their heads. When they move into adolescence and try to shout out their parents' voices, they have no internal "voice" of their own. So they begin to listen to other voices outside their heads — their peers' voices.

Drill sergeants frequently use punishment as a consequence of their teen's mistakes. However, the real world by and large doesn't operate by punishment. Unless they break the law and get convicted, adults don't get grounded when they mess up in life. And if they do experience some kind of punishment for their actions, they seldom pause for self-examination. Resentment is the more common reaction.

Drill sergeant parents eventually discover that when they punish their teens they provide them with a great escape valve: an escape from the consequences of their actions. Their teens never have to think when they're punished. All they do is seethe with resentment because parents are doing their thinking for them.

The real world doesn't operate on punishment. It operates on *consequences*. If we do a consistently lousy job at work, our boss doesn't take away our VCR. He fires us — and boy do we think of solutions then! In other words, we start saying, "I can think for myself."

Sometimes these two parenting styles, helicopters and drill sergeants, provide a cover for emotional distance from children. The family may live in the same house, eat at the same table, and ride in the same car, but they might as well be on different planets. Family members are often blind to the problem because they're not even aware it exists—and if they did have some vague sense of something being wrong, most likely they wouldn't be able to articulate it anyway.

When these families do interact on rare occasion, the parents fall into either the helicopter or drill sergeant style of relating to their children. It's either, "Oh, hon, you know we love you and will do anything for you"; or "Don't get emotional around me, buster; you do as you're told."

THE CONSULTANT PARENT

But helicopters can't hover forever. And eventually, drill sergeants go hoarse. Allow us to introduce a third alternative, employed by love-and-logic parents, which works well throughout life. However, it's especially effective with teenagers: the *consultant* parenting style.

In adolescence, an important change takes place in thinking ability. Children move from being "concrete" thinkers to having what noted child psychologist Jean Piaget called "formal operations" or abstract thinking. With this important change in cognition, parents must adjust the way they parent to meet the needs of the new thought processes happening in their children. (We will discuss this development at greater length in chapter 6.)

Children who think concretely need thoughtful guidance and sometimes firm limits. However, teens often resent guidelines and rebel at firm limits because they've grown to think differently.

Teens read the "rescue" message from helicopter parents as, "You're fragile and can't make it without me." And they pick up on the "do as I tell you" message from drill sergeant parents who covertly communicate, "You can't think for yourself, so I'll do it for you."

For many parents, setting limits turns into issuing commands. They back up those limits and rules with more commands—heavily spiced with sternness and anger—and when those fail they resort to punishment.

Typically, teens respond to these methods with irresponsibility, resistance, and rebellion.

Love-and-logic parents avoid the helicopter and drill sergeant mentalities by instead using a consultant style. They ask questions and offer choices. Instead of telling their children what to do, they put the burden of decision-making on their kids' shoulders. They establish options within limits.

Parents can prepare their children for the real world by shaping family life to reflect the realities their children will soon be facing on their own. Therefore, we can look to how consultants operate in other fields in order to enrich our understanding of a consultant parenting style.

Business Consultants
Businesses often hire specialized consultants to provide an outside perspective on a particular problem the company is facing. The company hires consultants for their expertise — *not* to tell the firm how to operate. In fact, the management of most businesses would fire a consultant who tries to order them around!

Consultants don't dictate, they *advise*. They say things like, "I'm wondering if it would be more effective for you to. . . ." This posture actually has great advantages, because consultants aren't responsible for whether their clients take their advice. If the client doesn't like the consultant's advice, the client doesn't have to listen to it anymore.

And neither are consultants responsible for what happens if their clients do take their advice. If a company loses money after following a consultant's recommendation, the loss isn't taken out of the consultant's pocket. Worst case, the consultant gets fired and loses referrals.

Therefore, as consultants give up authority, they happily give up the responsibility that accompanies it. That's an advantage!

Therapists and Guidance Counselors

A consulting example from another field is the therapist or the school guidance counselor. Here again, the consultant is sought out by the client.

Although young children do not decide on their own to consult a counselor (it's a rare eight-year-old who says, "Mommy, I need a therapist!"), most teens are able to recognize their own needs. Many of them will voluntarily and eagerly seek help from a guidance counselor or therapist.

Like business consultants, guidance counselors and therapists don't give orders. They don't ground anybody. They rarely get mad and shout at their clients. They seldom perform rescue missions, and they don't allow themselves to be manipulated or abused. But they do offer lots of empathy and understanding.

On the other hand, clients expect their counselors to be chock full of good ideas. Therapists and counselors are responsible for offering their own points of view while exploring those of their clients. They use paraphrasing and thoughtful silences. They may often look quizzical in response to what they're hearing. They may wonder aloud about possible alternatives.

But paramount to what therapists and counselors do for their clients involves their *attitude*. Most therapists feel that their clients are captains of their own ships of fate. They understand that their clients have made mistakes in the past and will most likely make mistakes in the future. Most therapists hope that their clients will listen to them but do not require it. They show great concern but are fairly slow to rescue. In fact, by law therapists are only allowed to rescue when persons are physically endangering themselves or others. That's a pretty narrow restriction!

Parents as Consultants

As children grow into adolescence, it is understandably difficult for many parents to make the shift from being a guide, or even a benevolent dictator, into becoming a consultant.

One of the biggest transitions is from "you" language to "I" language. Parents who have become consultants recognize that it's no longer helpful to send "you" messages such as, "John, you'd better get your homework done now." Instead, effective consultant parents use "I" messages that speak to their own wonderings, musings, and possible predictions:

- ◆ "I'm wondering if graduating from high school isn't too important to you."
- ◆ "I'm wondering if you feel upset with the choices you are making."
- ◆ "I'm curious about the feelings you're having that are leading you to the choices you're making."

These types of comments are far different from, "You'd better get that done this week if you want a grade for that paper."

Sadly, however, some parents of teens are still in the guide mode rather than the consultant mode. When confronted with their child's mistakes, they send the message, "What am *I* going to do now about *your* problem?" Regrettably, the "guide" parent takes on the teen's responsibility—which usurps the teen's ownership of his or her own problem.

Consultant parents live a much happier life. They put an arm around the teen and ask empathetically, "What a bummer! What are you going to do now?" This response places the responsibility of the decision squarely on the teen's shoulders.

There's a world of difference between the parent as guide and the parent as consultant. Being an effective consultant parent requires not only changes in the tools and techniques of parent-child interaction, but also a very important and basic shift in attitude. This is where love-and-logic parenting can make a major contribution to the teen's adjustment to the real world.

THE LOVE-AND-LOGIC WAY

We believe that one of the supreme goals of parenting is to raise responsible children — children who have been equipped with tools that will enable them to make wise choices throughout life.

The love-and-logic parenting style is based on a handful of core principles. Each principle is packed with underlying concepts and attitudes. They all work toward a simple method of raising children and helping teens become responsible and independent. We will explain the first three in greater detail in chapter 3, and the rest in chapter 4.

The following overview briefly summarizes the ideas that undergird this unique win-win approach for parents and their children.

Responsible Teens Feel Good About Themselves
Self-esteem doesn't just "happen" by making teens feeling good or happy. It begins when children assert their independence and try to show their families and the world that they are their own persons. But superficial trappings — looks, clothes, and a positive attitude — don't ensure that a teen will have a healthy self-concept. Teens develop this healthy self-concept through handling responsibility. In turn, they learn best when they feel good about themselves.

Responsibility Is Caught, Not Taught
Responsibility isn't something that a parent passes on to a teen by lectures, threats, or intimidation. Instead, responsibility and the self-esteem that goes along with it are passed on through covert messages that allow teens to build their

character on their strengths. We must give teens opportunities to make decisions—as well as mistakes.

Owning Up to Problems and Solutions
Here is an alternative to helicopter parents who constantly rescue their children from misfortunes and mistakes, and to drill sergeant parents who dress down their teens for goofing up: *Guide your teen to finding a solution to his or her own problem.* Love-and-logic consultant parents help their teens through life by offering choices, suggesting possible solutions to problems, and choosing to share control in the process.

Gaining Control Through Choices
It's only natural for parents to want to control their teens. But they must resist that natural urge if they want their teens to mature, and if they want to keep their sanity. Instead of viewing adolescence as a protracted conflict over control, why not loosen up a bit? The most effective parents are those who thoughtfully surrender control they don't have anyway by offering choices to their teens.

Setting Limits Through Thinking Words
Love-and-logic parents offer choices by using thinking words, not fighting words. They state what they will offer or allow; they don't dictate to their teen what to do. Thinking words make teens do the work to figure out the problem, while parents stand aside to see how their child performs.

Empathy Plus Consequences Equals Success
When teens falter, love-and-logic parents face the greatest obstacle and the greatest opportunity in watching their teen grow up. Instead of giving in to the temptation to rescue or get angry at the teen, love-and-logic parents empathize with their teen and allow the logical consequences of the teen's

mistake to sink in. Such empathy with consequences drives home the lesson that the parent loves the teen, but the teen needs to learn how the real world operates.

Build a Relationship to Last a Lifetime

These parenting techniques aren't just to help you work out the rough spots of raising teenagers. The goal is to guide your teen to live a responsible, productive, and happy life. By allowing your teen to achieve independence, you watch an adult blossom. And that adult, who happens to be your child, becomes your friend.

These principles form the basis for parenting teenagers with love and logic. We will explain them in greater detail in the next two chapters before we explore the special issues unique to teenagers.

3
BACK TO THE BASICS, PART ONE:
Training Teens to Act Responsibly

❖

L ove-and-logic parenting is built on a group of principles that can be applied to children of any age
for training them to act responsibly. In this and the
following chapter we present these building blocks with
special applications to teenagers, so by the time they are sixteen or seventeen, they are able to make their own decisions,
find their way in the world, and become the responsible
kind of adults you would want as your friends.

BASIC SELF-CONCEPT — WHO AM I?

John's best buddy came up to him at lunch and said, "Hey,
John, I've got this really great stuff. Let's go smoke some of
it behind the school."

"Sure, why not?" John replied. No "Just Say No" campaign had ever bothered him.

But John's dad—who wasn't even there—bothered John. *Boy,* he said to himself, *if I do that, my dad will really get mad.* And what's the next thing John said to himself? *Oh, he'll never find out.*

Teens are full of bravado, swagger, words, threats, intimidation, and voices—loud voices coming from outside their heads. But even in the best of situations, teens naturally suffer many problems with self-concept and doubt.

For all his supposed independence, John had a crummy way of making a decision. When sensible teens are asked to do drugs, they say to themselves, *Hey, I wonder how this is going to affect me?*

Teens struggle with many things in their lives that they don't understand. It's natural for them to go through some pretty shaky times, but those will pass. What's important is that they gain a strong self-concept that will not only get them through tomorrow but give them stability for the future as well.

Frankie, for instance, doesn't have the stability that his parents do, with their marriage, house, and cars. Frankie doesn't know who he is yet, but he's working like crazy to find out. So he spends a lot of time away from home at Bill's to compare ratty jeans and earrings and prove to himself that he's not just an extension of his home. He spends increasing time listening to Bill to show that he's not always listening to the folks. It doesn't occur to Frankie that he's still listening to somebody *outside* his head—it's just that now the voice is more often Bill's than his parents.

Adolescent identity crises occur when teens are trying to make the right choices but they can't figure out whether it's because they want to or because it makes their parents happy. This is the classic adolescent identity crisis that James Dean immortalized in *Rebel Without a Cause.*

Self-Concept Struggles in Adolescence

Self-concept is usually at its lowest ebb during the teenage years because so many things are happening that are very difficult to understand.

Every time teens look at their bodies, for example, they end up disappointed. There's something wrong with their hair. Their friends dress better than they do. Their body shape is too big or too small. They keep asking themselves, *What does a "normal" teenager look like? How does a "normal" teenager act?*

These questions drive teens crazy, continually throwing their self-concept into doubt. And wise parents know that teens' fears about themselves are often at their height just when they're acting the most sure of themselves.

What happens with friendships during those times? "Gee, my friend liked me yesterday but now he hates me. . . . The girls used to include me until I started hanging out with so-and-so." The cliques change constantly.

More important than appearances or friendships, however, are the life-and-death issues confronting teens on a daily basis. Possible abuse at home, drugs, and suicide push and pull on them. If their self-concept isn't secure, they could stumble — with fatal results.

Tracking the Causes of Damaged Self-Concept

Problems with self-concept often start in the first year or two of life. Most parents don't intentionally damage their child's self-concept, but it can happen in many ways:

- ◆ Excessive criticism.
- ◆ Overprotection and/or overindulgence.
- ◆ Neglect.
- ◆ Perfectionism.
- ◆ Genetics and/or prenatal factors.
- ◆ Excessive or inadequate control.
- ◆ Pushing children into formal learning before they're ready.

◆ Comparing children to others who are better
  achievers.
◆ Failure to allow children to own their own rewards
  and disappointments.
◆ Conditional love.
◆ Allowing children to be disrespectful.
◆ Failure of parents to provide an adequate model of
  taking good care of oneself.
◆ Learning disabilities.
◆ Emotional problems.
◆ Lack of early bonding.

When you read this list of what can damage self-concept, you may wonder how good a parent you've been. No one bats a thousand — we've all made some mistakes. But you do have a choice about what you will do with the future. You can decide which attitudes will make you happiest and which will make your child — now a teenager — happiest.

Minute-to-Minute Self-Concept Building
Teens look to us for positive or negative affirmations. They store them in their memory banks. The perceptions gained from these parental messages actually become the teens' reality. Here are some tips we can remember to raise the odds for success as we exercise our responsibility to build the self-concept of our teens:

1. Provide both stated and unstated messages that show you have unconditional love.
2. Model your own healthy self-concept to your teen.
3. Provide both stated and unstated messages that say, "I value you."
4. Provide both stated and unstated messages that say, "You can think."
5. Provide both stated and unstated messages that say, "You have control."

6. Provide opportunities for teens to struggle through and own their own decisions and responsibilities.

Three ways to show love are eye contact, touching, and smiles. In combination with each other, they're dynamite. The way we listen to teens also greatly affects how loved they feel and how much they love us.

We'd like to be able to help our kids. But ironically, this strong desire to help and care for other people can become our worst enemy in caring for our teens. If this desire leads to overprotection, it will thwart opportunities for teens to learn responsibility.

The Three Voices of Self-Concept

Self-concept is like a three-legged table. If all three aspects of self-concept are not in place, it is wobbly. These three legs are like three voices. Teens with a strong self-concept have three voices in their ear.

The first voice says, "I'm loved by the magic people in my life" — the significant other people. We're all magic people in the lives of teens.

The second voice says, "I have just as many skills as I need for a person my age. I can compete in the classroom. I can compete at home. I can compete out on the street. I can compete in sports. I can compete anywhere with people my age. I'm okay."

The third voice says, "I can take control of my life. I can take responsibility and make decisions for myself, and [here's the important part] I can live with the consequences of my decisions or actions."

LOVE-AND-LOGIC PRINCIPLE: RESPONSIBLE TEENS
FEEL GOOD ABOUT THEMSELVES

Responsibility isn't something that a parent passes on to a teen by lectures, threats, or intimidation. Responsibility and its companion, self-concept, are passed on through covert messages that allow teens to build their character on their strengths. As we give teens opportunities to make decisions, we must also allow them to make mistakes.

Love-and-logic parenting techniques rely in part on a worn-out phrase: "Children learn best and kids develop responsibility best when they feel good about themselves." Conversely, children who are not responsible do not have a good self-concept. Healthy teens can say to themselves, "I can take care of my life. I can take control of my life."

However, this philosophy does not define giving children responsibility as letting them get away with unacceptable behavior. Parents have a perfect right to expect responsible behavior from their children.

This philosophy also says that adults and teens grow by building on their strengths. But that isn't the way many of us grew up.

When I (Jim) went to school, if a teacher had asked me, "Hey, Jimmy! What are you good at?" I would've said, "I don't know." And if the teacher pressed me, "Well, who *does* know?" then I would have answered, "Well, my teacher, my mother. They're supposed to know things like that."

But what if they came in and said, "Hey, Jimmy! What are your weaknesses?" Boy, I was an expert on that. I could rattle those things off because my teachers and my parents felt that before I could learn anything, I had to realize how weak I was. For example, every time I turned around, my mother was saying to me, "Jim, your speech is sloppy. Watch your M's, P's, and B's." But this ongoing critique didn't really help me. And I think I'm no different from anybody else.

Let's help teens become aware of their strengths and build from there. But this doesn't mean that we should ignore their weaknesses. They can and should be working on them. But my rule is: *I will never require myself, or one of my children, to work on more than one weakness at a time.*

Covert Messages

The strongest messages we pick up from people are the implied ones, not the actual words that are said. These are what we've been calling "covert" messages.

When we imply to teens that they can handle a situation, they handle it. And when we imply to them that they can't handle it, they don't. When we send teens a subconscious message that they can think, their self-concept improves. If teens receive enough of those good messages, that learn to like themselves.

The connection can be put in terms of a self-fulfilling prophecy: "I don't become what *you* think I can, and I don't become what *I* think I can. I become what *I think* you think I can."

Have you ever had a boss, a friend, or a teacher who thought you were the greatest thing going? How did you perform around that person? Did you make weekly appointments to go in and say, "Now, wait a minute. I'm not as good as you think I am"? Or did you find yourself living up to those expectations? Have you ever been around a person who thought you were the scum of the earth? How did that affect your responses?

A lot of our parenting work centers around how we can imply to teens — that means without directly saying it — that we know they're going to handle whatever life hands them. Then we must trust them to do it and allow that self-fulfilling prophecy to come into play.

Just as there are parents who imply that a teen is either great or scum, there are two kinds of teens, too.

Sarah wakes up in the morning, marches into the bathroom, and says to the mirror, "Hey, look at that babe. She's all right. I like that woman, and I bet other people are going to like her, too."

Now switch to Linda. She wakes up in the morning, drags herself over to the mirror, and mumbles to herself, "Oh, no, look at that. I don't like what I see. And I'll bet other people don't like her either."

Which of those teens causes problems at home or in school? Linda, of course. She looks at herself and pronounces, "I'm bad." What comes next? "Bad teens should be punished. So how come nobody punishes me?" Then she hooks somebody into it: "I'll do something bad, and if they don't punish me, I'll do something worse." When she finally gets punished she can say, "See? I'm bad, and I should be punished."

Which covert messages do you want to send? The ones that prompt your teen to respond, "Oh, yeah? Make me do it," or the ones that invite your teen to comply, and feel good about it?

LOVE-AND-LOGIC PRINCIPLE: RESPONSIBILITY IS CAUGHT, NOT TAUGHT

Parents have this much in common with God: We can give our children considerable freedom, just as God gave it to all humans—his supreme creation. This means freedom to goof up as well as get it right. Failure and success are two sides of the same coin.

For children to make their own decisions they will sometimes have to assert independence by consciously choosing to fail. Paradoxically, then, *parents who try to ensure their children's successes often raise unsuccessful children.*

One thing we definitely cannot make teens do is "be responsible." Responsibility cannot be *taught*; it must be *caught*. The hardest lessons to learn involve the things we're told we *must* do. To help our children gain responsibility we must *offer them opportunities* to be responsible.

"Rules" as such don't do much for building responsibility, because rules and regulations vary from job to job, institution to institution. Sometimes there are no rules at all—or only dumb rules.

I (Foster) heard about one western university that laid

down a new rule a few years ago: no sex in the coed dorms. That's a dumb rule. Most of us feel that sex should not be allowed in *any* of the dorms.

But let's say Jerry enters Behemoth Western University. He's eighteen years old and always has done what Mom and Dad told him to do. When he hits campus he thinks, *Gosh, I've never seen so many beautiful girls in my life.* He calls his folks after the first week and says, "Hey, Mom and Dad! These girls here are awesome! I'm going out with one to a party tomorrow night!"

Now guess what happens. Mom and Dad—speaking long distance—try to enforce the university's "no-sex-in-the-dorms" rule: "Now Jerry, just where are you going to be tonight? Will there be any drugs there? When are you going to be back in your room? We want you back at twelve, and we don't mean one minute past twelve."

"Sure Mom, sure Dad," Jerry assures them. "I'll be good, just like you told me to." Maybe he even *means* it.

Come midnight when the beer is passed around, Jerry has a choice to make. He can listen to the memories of his parents or yield to the encouragement of his buddies and the girl tugging on his arm. But Jerry has never had the choice of listening to himself and making up his own mind.

Honestly now, do "no-sex-in-the-dorm-rooms" rules make any sense at all? Of course not.

The only way any meaningful, mature behavior happens is when it springs from within our teen's character. And character is formed through learning to make decisions and learning to live with the consequences. We parents were able to get away with making choices for our children when they were young and didn't necessarily need to feel the sting of the consequences from their bad choices. That may have been easy for us as parents then, but if we keep it up it's not going to be easy for teens who confront literal life-and-death decisions almost unheard of a generation or two ago.

Tragically, for many teens the first real decisions they

make are foolish choices about cars, sex, or behavior on the job. If they never had the opportunity to make decisions and own the consequences, it really doesn't matter what they learned in driver education or health classes—because *they never learned responsibility.*

Responsibility is caught when parents share control with their teens. We can encourage teenagers to think for themselves while we help their self-concept stay intact. When teens think on their own, they make choices and learn to live with the consequences. If those consequences mean that they learn life's lessons the hard way, we can provide an equal amount of empathy or sadness to go along with it. That drives the pain of the consequence home so that they never forget the lesson.

Shortly after Jerry went to the campus party, his loving parents were called. Jerry, it seems, had gotten into trouble. Not only was he arrested for public intoxication, he also was caught escorting the girl—whose name he had quickly forgotten—out of his dorm at 6 a.m. the next morning.

Now it's Jerry's parents' turn to make a decision:

They can yell at Jerry, "We told you to be back in your room by midnight, but you didn't listen! We're really mad at you! It'll cost us fifty dollars for your court costs and the fine for being drunk in public."

Or, they can realize that Jerry is on his own now and must make his own decisions: "Well, son, we're truly sorry about what happened. We know that you really needed that money to buy some school books instead of pay that fine, but we're sure you can find a part-time job in the evenings to make it up. Best of luck for the rest of the term."

Few teens really want to stay teenagers forever. They want to grow up and assert their independence, even if they show it in superficial ways. They've got the clothes, the swagger, and the answers. So let them act independent—and then let them live with what they've decided. Because, in a few very short years, they won't have you to bail them out when they total the car, argue with their spouse, or squander the rent money for their apartment. Why wait?

Some of us wait because of deeply ingrained patterns of parenting from that long-ago era when our sixteen-year-old hell-raiser was just a cute little devilish imp. We wanted to do everything humanly possible for our little one. But what got us into trouble was *how we showed our "love"* — often as protectionism.

Parents who don't know any better tend to fall into the "helicopter" and "drill sergeant" parenting styles that we've already seen don't work.

LOVE-AND-LOGIC PRINCIPLE: LET TEENS OWN THEIR PROBLEMS AND THEIR SOLUTIONS

Love-and-logic consultant parents help teens through life by offering choices and sharing control in the process, all the while building on teens' healthy self-concept. They let teens own their problems as well as their solutions.

Building a strong self-concept is the first of three things we can do with teens so when they reach the age of temptation, we've got a chance that they're not going to abuse drugs and alcohol.

The second thing we can do is to help teens learn how to make decisions. We do this in part by letting them own the responsibility — including the good feelings as well as the disappointments — of those decisions, planting in their consciousness the idea, "The quality of my life depends on the decisions I make."

Third, we can make it clear who owns the responsibility for a particular problem. If parents don't draw clear lines of demarcation when they're called for, they and their teenagers are in for a lot of grief.

Let the teens own their own problems, their own feelings, their own disappointments, their own rewards. One of the worst things we can do is give teens the message that they shouldn't do something because the logical consequence of their action is to make adults mad. First, that encourages them to shape their actions according to the voices outside their heads. And second, it can reinforce an immature rebellion in some teens who will go out of their way to make adults mad. Either way, they don't own the situation.

For example, let's say your daughter is out driving the family car and she's tempted to show off for her friends. Should she be thinking, "Boy, if I crash this car, my dad's really going to be mad"? Is that how a mature teen would react?

If she's a sensible young woman on her way to healthy independence, that's not what she'll be thinking. Instead, she will say to herself, "Gee, if I crash this car, I'm going to splatter us all over the highway. Guess I better be careful."

It's the teen's responsibility to own the problem and find a solution. But that's not always as easy as it sounds, because we're tempted to rush in like a helicopter to protect our son or daughter from the real world. Or we march in like a drill sergeant, bark a few orders, and expect the teenage troops to fall into line unquestioningly. Those temptations must be resisted.

As a person in the helping profession of education, I (Jim) feel tempted to solve my students' problems. So I've trained myself to do something different by using a key word: *bummer.* Whenever I use that word, it reminds me: "Jim, be careful. Don't solve the problem for him. Don't give him a solution. Don't give him advice, and don't be defensive. Let *him* do the thinking." And when the student hears "bummer," it sounds empathetic. "Gee, too bad. Bummer. I bet that feels lousy."

If we show that we understand how teens feel, we hand their feelings back to them—for *their* control, not ours.

Ownership of problems also founders on confusing

praise and *encouragement.* For the past ten years in public schools, we've heard about something called "positive reinforcement." That philosophy says that if we spend a lot of time telling teens how well they're doing, they will do better.

This approach works well with teens who see themselves as a "10" because they don't have to search for proof to back up their self-image. But how many teens in our classrooms or homes really consider themselves "10"s?

We can encourage teens best by talking to them as adults. We do *not* build self-concept by telling them they're good. Teens with a poor self-image will simply discount it, and they'll probably end up worse off than if we'd said nothing.

One day teens are down; the next day they're up. It goes with the territory. We can help by criticizing them as little as possible and by refraining from telling them what they should be discovering for themselves. We want them to think for themselves, so we should be asking them questions instead of ordering them around. When they say they're going to do something stupid, we can respond, "Well, that's an option. You can do that. Have you ever thought of this, this, and this? We wish you well, and we'll still love you no matter what happens."

By talking to teens as if they were adults, we convey the strong message that we expect them to act like adults and take charge of things in their lives. But we certainly don't do this by lectures or threats.

In the next chapter, we'll examine how to speak to teens effectively through the following love-and-logic principles:

◆ Gaining control through choices.
◆ Setting limits through thinking words.
◆ The recipe for success: empathy with consequences.
◆ Building a relationship to last a lifetime.

4
BACK TO THE BASICS, PART TWO:
Treating Teenagers as Responsible Adults

❖

Fourteen-year-old Tina was angry and confused. Her mom, she said, treated her like she was either a two-year-old or an adult.

"Mom treats me okay when she's talking to me about my clothes, my friends, or my homework—those things are okay," Tina explained. "But when she's telling me if I can date or who can be my boyfriend, it's like I'm a little girl who doesn't know anything."

Tina's mom wasn't too happy either. "Tina acts like either a young lady or a two-year-old. I can't figure her out! She's so sweet when I ask how school is going, or when she shows off her new dress. But when we talk about those boys with the weird haircuts she likes, who I think are bad influences on her, she practically throws tantrums."

Tina and her mom were locked in a typical parental battle over control. On things the mom felt weren't too consequential, such as clothes, friends, and schoolwork, then Tina was a young adult. But when it came to Tina's choice of boyfriends and dating, her mom treated her like she was two. The more her mom pressed those issues, the more Tina rebelled—which is the same issue parents face with two-year-olds.

LOVE-AND-LOGIC PRINCIPLE: GAINING CONTROL THROUGH CHOICES

Have you, like Tina's mom, noticed the strong desire to enforce tighter rules with your teen? When you start to see your teen becoming independent, your natural tendency is to say, "I'd be a better parent if I could only control. . . ."

But we have free will, and that means the right to make lots of decisions and live with the consequences. That's what makes human beings exciting! Wouldn't it be terrible if we *could* control our children's every move? Can you imagine the kind of people we'd have to live with when they grew up? At best, it would be awfully boring!

Would you like your teen to be reasonable, fun to be around, and responsible as well? Then *relax your grip.* Remember that your teen will be out in the adult world a few short years from now, so *share control.* The more control *you relinquish* now, the more *they gain* now. That's the *self-control* that they will use to make quality decisions in establishing themselves as adults. The happiest teens are responsible teens who operate under real world rules that inspire self-control rather than under parental rules and control that may encourage rebellion.

But *how* do we share control? Have you ever watched the classic scene of a parent trying to get absolute control, and in the next split second the teen gets total control? What goes wrong?

In human interaction, there's a very fine line here. On one side of the line, the teens feel that they have some control. But on the other side of the line, they have none. Once we cross over onto the side where teens feel they have no control, that's when they suddenly decide to get it all.

For example, Dad warns his son, "You be home at midnight or else." The teen has no control over the situation. At that point, however, he can take total control by deciding to come home after midnight, and Dad must then react to *him*.

Achieving the Right Mix of Control

Psychologist Sylvia B. Rimm, Ph.D., states that people of all ages compare the amount of control they have in a relationship only to the amount of control they *used to* have — not to the amount they feel they *should* have. When more control is expanded over time, people are satisfied; when control is cut back, people are angry. Therefore, when parents relinquish control in increasing amounts, children — especially teenagers — are usually satisfied with the level of control.

Dr. Rimm's analysis is called the "V" of love. The sides of the "V" represent firm limits within which the child may make decisions and live with the consequences. The bottom of the "V" represents birth, while the top represents the time when the child leaves home for adult life.[1] Examples of relinquishing control might be giving toddlers the choice of white or chocolate milk; for teens, it may be the opportunity to decide when they will come home at night.

Unfortunately, many parents turn the "V" upside down. They treat their children like miniature adults right from the start, with all the privileges of adulthood granted immediately at birth. These children soon become tyrants. The parents don't control them; they control their parents, holding them hostage with temper tantrums and pouting. Tragically, many children who begin life with too much power lead unhappy lives as they grow older. Their misbehavior as teens forces parents to keep clamping down on them, triggering anger and rebellion as rights and privileges are forcibly withdrawn. The unhappy teen then complains, "You're treating me like a five-year-old." And in many ways, that's true.

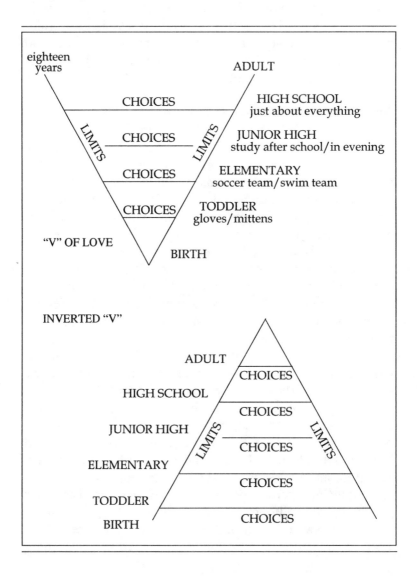

Rules for Control Battles

The love-and-logic approach to control says, "Don't be greedy. Never take any more control than you absolutely need to have." When the threat of a battle for control looms on the horizon, parents must ask themselves some questions, such as, "How much control do I absolutely need in this situation? More important than that, do I need to fight a control battle at all? Can my teen learn a valuable lesson if I offer advice or options instead?"

Love-and-logic parents have learned that the more they relax, the easier it is to deal with control. We recommend three rules for control battles:

1. Avoid control battles at all costs.

2. If you are forced to have a control battle—on those rare occasions when it can't be avoided—then win it at all costs.

3. Pick the issue carefully and deliberately without threatening to do so. Just do it.

When effective parents use these techniques, they don't have a battle. Instead, they cause teens to think about their decisions.

When parents do get into control battles, teens are thinking about one thing: *Who's going to win?* They're especially good at picking battles that adults can't ever win: "What music are you going to forbid me to listen to? Who are you going to allow to be my boyfriends/girlfriends? When am I going to learn? See if you can make me talk. See if you can make me happy." These are the common battlegrounds for parents and teens.

Whenever parents give teens an order that they can't enforce, they lose their teens' respect. Control battles over friends is an example. If I say to my daughter, "Don't go out with that friend" or "I don't like those friends; don't hang around them," I'm giving her an order that I can't make her follow. I'm starting a battle I will inevitably lose. Why? My daughter is growing more independent as she enters adolescence, and choosing her own friends is one way of expressing that independence. No way will I be able to monitor her behavior twenty-four hours a day. Practically speaking, I couldn't enforce such a control battle even if I tried—so why not save the energy for one I can win?

But your teen might very well find that such a control battle is something she wants you to fight. Little children, not to mention teenagers, discover that they can bring great big adults to their knees with no effort whatsoever. All they need to do is trick the adults into fighting some kind of a battle that could never be won in a million years. Then they keep the adults busy fighting that battle. And the adults have neither the time nor the energy left to fight the more important battles they could have won.

There are, however, a few issues over which you must have control battles because they center around your self-respect as a parent. Choose these battles carefully, with every intention to win them. They include:

1. Parents must insist on respect from their children, even as their children deserve respect from their parents. When children are disrespectful of their parents, it lowers their self-image. Poor self-image starts with disrespect of parents.

2. Parents must exert control over basic conduct in family life. For example, if a teen is disturbing parents by smoking in the house, parents must model their self-respect and tell him or her to step outside. It's generally a mistake to get into a physical tussle with the teen, but parents can say in a firm "we mean business" voice, "We think you're making an unwise decision." They might not be able to remove the teen at that moment, but they must be able to establish that limit.

3. Parents must have control of the home environment. After all, the parents *do* own the home. Sometimes teens bring whomever they wish into the home and act as if they own the house. That's backwards. Who owns the

environment is an important concept. When the children grow up and have their own home, then they will have the right to make decisions in that environment.

John and his father used to get into continual battles around the stereo system. John would slip in a disk, turn it up loud, and his music would literally pound through the home. Then John's father would inevitably yell, over the din, "Turn that blankety-blank stereo down!" John would take his time about complying and then sit and pout in a rebellious manner.

After attending a parenting seminar, John's father handled it differently. He waited for the microsecond that he and John were both in a great mood. Then he sat down with his son, literally putting his arm around his shoulders (this action was so rare that it shocked John into focused awareness), and said, "You know, John, I understand how you love your music. And, I admit, I have a hard time enjoying it. So, I would really like you to keep the volume low when you play music on the main stereo when Mom and I are home."

"Well, it seems unfair. You get to play your music up loud. This is my home too!" John answered.

"John," his father said lovingly, "you need to check the mortgage, find out whose home this is. This is my home, son. However, you get to live here. Someday, when you make the mortgage payments on your own home, I won't expect to bring over my disk and say, 'Hey, stuff this sucker into the machine and turn it up loud.' You know what I mean?"

John replied—a little resistant, but with dawning awareness—"Yeah, I guess that makes sense."

Dad ended the conversation by saying, "I'll do my best not to feel too resentful of your music, and I would really appreciate your doing your best to keep down the decibels. Thanks a lot, John."

He gave his son a little squeeze around the shoulders and left. By his father's loving limits John was shocked into an awareness that the kids really *don't* own the home.

Try These Control Battles on for Size

Teens pick some interesting battles to wage, including: "See if you can make me talk." Good luck! I (Jim) remember when my second daughter was a teenager, the hours of energy we put into, "Now I can see there's something wrong. Why don't you talk about it? What's the matter? You know you can talk to us. You know it's safe to talk to us." And the more we said "talk," the less she said because her silence put her in control.

Another battle that teenagers love to engage us in concerns values: "See if you can make me have the same values you have." Again, lots of luck. The truth is that healthy teenagers, as a normal part of growing up, are constantly trying out some new value: "Would this be okay? Would that be okay?" They're experimenting with becoming adults.

This is why teens often make blunt statements such as, "School's not important." Then they stand back to watch their parents go crazy. It's not uncommon in this day and age for teens to come home and say, "I think anybody ought to be able to have sex with anybody they want, anytime, anyplace. And it's nobody's business, especially their parents'."

Parents inevitably respond to statements like these by immediately trying to correct them: "Oh no, don't believe that, believe this. This will help, and that will help, and you can't do that." The teen subconsciously revels in the parents' fumbling attempts to respond to his or her new values. Somewhere inside, the teen is saying, "Good luck. That will keep you busy for a while—so busy you won't have time to win some battles you could have won."

What's so sad about this situation? These parents have just caused their teen to hold on for dear life to that particular value, because now that position is a way for the teen to establish who he or she is as an individual apart from the parents.

A better response is to allow teens to try on that new

value. You can be sure they will come up with something else next month or next week.

But some parents can't let go of the anxiety: "What if my kid comes home and says something off the wall, like, communism is a really great way to distribute wealth and create just societies? How do I handle that?" Look at your teen, smile, and say, "Thanks for sharing that. I've always wondered how teenagers see that."

Let's play this out a little further and see what happens.

"But don't you see, Mom?" he continues. "Wouldn't it be wonderful if all the rich people could share their stuff with poor people?"

"Well, son," Mom responds, "that sounds interesting, but what if rich people don't want to go along with that?"

"Well, maybe people in power would have to force them to give up what they have."

"Oh, like you have your stereo, and Dad and I don't have a stereo," Mom observes. "So we'd make you give us your stereo, right?"

Then Mom does a little of what we call referential speaking, in which parents refer to their values without forcing them on teens. She concludes, "That sure wouldn't work for us in our country, but I can understand how a teen would see it that way." This response forces teens to think: *Wait a minute! Mom's not playing the game right. She should be fighting over that.*

Parents often don't know this, but patience is one of the best qualities for enduring a values battle. Long before your teens turn thirty, they will wake up and discover that they hold many of the same values as you do! So if they've had a good first eleven years of life, it really doesn't matter what they say about their values during the teenage years. By the time they're adults, they'll pretty well share your values.

The third big control battle with teens is, "See if you can make me learn." That only happens in families where the parents have made it very clear: "We're going to make you learn." When parents throw down such a gauntlet, they inevitably have control battles about homework, grades, and extracurricular activities—all the way to dating and curfews. And of course, parents will lose those battles while the teens' grades are sliding along with their respect for their parents.

Love-and-logic parents don't worry about *making* their teens learn. First, they know they can't control whether or not their teens study. Second, the grades are the *teen's* grades, not the parents' grades. These parents have made it clear to their children that their success in school is *their* responsibility. The teens own their success, or they own their laziness. In those families, teens usually say to themselves, "Boy, if they're not going to worry about it, somebody had better worry—namely, me."

How to Offer Teens Choices

The most effective parents are always thoughtfully surrendering control by offering their teens choices.

The best time to give teens choices is when things are going well instead of waiting until things are falling apart. You'll come out ahead if you give choices rather than orders. Many really effective parents create a type of "savings account" in the teen's mind that he or she has plenty of control by giving them many choices when things are going really well. Then when things aren't going well, the parents can say, "Wait a minute, kid. It's my turn!"

This love-and-logic technique can be compared to poker. Life is a game of poker in which parents hold all the aces. The parents lay down aces for major events in their teen's life, such as learning to drive. But the parents can always say, "I call."

Have you ever looked into a teen's eyes while you're saying "shut up!" or "turn that stereo down"? What happens? They twinkle with anticipation, don't they? The teen says, "All right! Let's get it on, here we go." In other words, *any time we tell teens to do something we can't make them do, we give them too much control.*

Here is where you must offer choices. Always start out very nicely with, "Would you rather?" or "What would be best for you?" or "Feel free to." You might say, "Feel free to make all the noise you want somewhere else," or "Feel free to stay here and be quiet. You decide."

Most creative teens will come up with a third choice, and we're not always going to like it, so brace yourself. That third choice often carries the response, "I live here. I've got rights. I can make noise because this is my house, too."

No matter what third choice teens come up with, we must be ready with this rehearsed response: "What were the choices?" And the teen will say, "Yeah, but I—this isn't fair. My friends don't have to put up with that."

We say again in a very soft voice, which doesn't get any louder, "What were the choices?"

The teen says, "This is dumb!"

We say, "What were the choices?" Or another alternative, "What did I say?"—always in a nice tone.

Most normal teens, after they hear "What were the choices?" three or four times, will respond, "Give me a break, how long—what do I have to do to get away from this crazy adult?" In other words, we have the right to drive our teens crazy, too!

Whenever you can, *set your teen in a situation where he or she can't say no, but instead must make some kind of decision.*

Love-and-logic parents don't waste time saying, "You can't do this, you can't do that." Instead, they say things like, "How are you going to handle it when . . . ?"

Some Tips on Choices
Don't turn choices into threats by telling your teen, "Choose my way—or else." Here's a supposed choice that is actually a thinly veiled threat: "You can either do your chores or lose your right to the car." That's no different from the

boss saying, "Would you rather do that report today or get fired?" We must offer real and realistic choices, not threats. For example:

- ◆ "Would you rather clean your room or mow the lawn so I'll have time to clean your room?"
- ◆ "Would you rather wash the car this morning or this afternoon?"
- ◆ "Do you want to negotiate a reasonable time to come home at night or not go out at all?"

Non-threatening choices, offered calmly, give teens a chance to take some control over their lives.

In summary, as we offer choices to our teens, we should remember five basic points:

1. Select only those choices that you as a parent like. Never offer one you like together with one you don't like, because instinctively teens will usually select the one you don't like.

2. Never give a choice unless you are willing to allow your teen to experience the consequences of that choice.

3. Never give choices when the teen is in danger.

4. Never give choices unless you are willing to make the choice in the event the teen doesn't.

5. Pay careful attention to your delivery. Try to start your sentence with one of the following:

"You're welcome to _____ or _____."
"Feel free to _____ or _____."
"Would you rather _____ or _____?"
"What would be best for you— _____ or _____?"

LOVE-AND-LOGIC PRINCIPLE: SHARING CONTROL THROUGH THINKING WORDS

Remember helicopter and drill sergeant parents? When they talk to their teens, they either smother them with overprotection or hand down angry orders. In either case, teens resent that sort of talk because it makes them feel like children. So it always sounds like fighting words to them.

Instead of the fighting words of helicopter and especially drill sergeant parents, love-and-logic parents use *thinking words*. They send the message to their teens, "*You'd better think* because the quality of your life has a lot to do with your decisions."

Teens will believe something that comes from inside their own heads. When they choose an option, they do the thinking, they make the choice, and the lesson sticks with them.

Consultant parents also take really good care of themselves in front of their teenagers when they're teaching them to think. The parents affirm, "If my kid is ever going to grow up to learn how to take care of herself, she had better see it in action."

One way we do this is by telling teens what *we're* going to do, not what *they're* going to do. Telling teens what *they're* going to do is a waste of time and energy. They'll just get angry. Telling them what *we're* going to do confuses them. That beats anger every time.

One of the best ways to help yourself in such situations is to use the phrase "no problem." That is, what you decide to do is no problem for you, but it might be a problem for your teen.

A woman wrote to us and told us the results of using the trigger term, "no problem":

My kids think the phrase "no problem" has something to do with them. But it has something to do with me. It reminds me to use my techniques. So when the kids get upset, I say, "No problem, right?"

The other thing I learned was never tell the kid what to do. I tell him what *I'm* going to do."

It really worked on my fourteen-year-old, Tony.

For years, I'd had trouble with him every Saturday morning. I'd try to get him to clean up his room by saying to him, "I'm not driving you to your soccer game until you get that room cleaned; so do it *now!*" And he would always play brain drain on me.

"Brain drain" is trying to get an adult to do all the thinking, all the defending, and all the reasoning. As soon as the adult responds the teen just sits back and subconsciously says, *It won't work. You don't love me. You don't care.* This woman explained to us:

> Well, Tony would always say things like, "You don't care if the team wins? What is the coach going to think? The other kids are really going to think that I let them down. You don't want me to let the other kids down, do you?"
> I would always end up driving him to the game, screaming at him about the room, and being unhappy. I couldn't enjoy the game.

Eventually, she learned how to say "no problem" and discovered how to tell him what *she* would do, not what *he* had to do:

> So I went to him and said, "Tony, I'm going to drive you to your game just as soon as you vacuum your room."
> "Vacuuming is woman's work," he answered me.
> I had to actually hold on to the table while I said, "No problem, Tony"!
> "What do you mean, no problem?"
> "I just mean that I guess it isn't going to be a problem for me anymore." I went to the phone and called up a friend so that I wouldn't have to talk to him, because I didn't have any more answers.

Ten minutes later I heard the vacuum running. I really didn't recognize it at first because, you know, I've never heard it from a distance.

What I discovered through this was that before, when I was telling him what to do he had something to fight. But when I told him what *I* was going to do instead, he was only confused. It's interesting and rewarding to watch fourteen-year-olds a bit confused and, at the same time, learning how to grow up.

Parents of teenagers know that teens fight commands, because they see an implied threat in them. They also know that some teens respond to threats and others don't.

"Fighting words" invite disobedience. Here are some examples:

- When we tell our teens what to do. ("Clean out the garage, *now*.")
- When we tell our teens what we will not allow. ("I won't let you hang out with that biker gang.")
- When we tell our teens what we won't do for them. ("I'm not driving you to the dance until you finish your homework."

When we issue these kinds of commands we're calling our teens to battles — mostly to ones we can't win.

Instead, love-and-logic parents make statements with *thinking words*, telling our teens:

- What we will allow. ("Feel free to join us for the next meal as soon as the lawn is mowed.")
- What we will do. ("I'll be thrilled to give you a driving lesson as soon as you've chopped the wood.")
- What we will provide. ("You may watch the TV show the rest of the family is watching, or you

may wait until we're through and find something on another channel that pleases you more.")

When we give our children the right to make decisions, there is no anger for them to rebel against. Nobody's doing their thinking for them, and the limit is established.

Also, our choices must make real-world sense. As your teens edge closer to the time they'll fly the nest, it's important to stress, "Well honey, that's the way the world works for me. First, I get my job done, then I get paid, then I eat. If it's good enough for me, guess who else it's good enough for?"

Gold or Garbage?
Is my word "gold" or "garbage" when I say to you, "Don't you look at me like that! And don't you talk to me like that! You get a civil tongue in your mouth!" Can I enforce that? No! So my word is garbage.

Am I expressing *wishes* or *limits*? Here I'm expressing wishes because I'm talking about you, and I can't control you. There's one person in the world I have control over: me. If I want to set limits and turn my words into gold, I must absolutely talk about me, and what I would be glad to do.

Parents who turn their word into gold always talk about what they will offer, what they will allow, and what they will put up with. They seldom tell teens what to do.

"I'll be glad to listen to you when your voice is as soft as mine. Take your time. I'll see you later." Now, did I express a wish or a limit there? Did I have to raise my voice? Did I have to add on, "I mean it"? Did I have to add, "Or else"? I become very powerful when I talk about me. I become powerless and impotent when I talk about what you have to do.

For example, I say, "As long as you live in this house, you're not going to drink. Don't test me! I really mean it this time." It's a wish for my teen, isn't it? But instead I say: "Would it be reasonable that if I don't have to worry about your using alcohol, then I wouldn't have to worry about your using the car when it's available? Have we got a deal? Put 'er there." Am I frowning or smiling? Smiling. Am I talking about something I can control or something I cannot control? Something I can control, of course.

LOVE-AND-LOGIC PRINCIPLE: CONSEQUENCES AND SORROW

The old (and still popular) technique for control was anger, lectures, threats, and intimidation. The love-and-logic technique is equal parts of *consequence* and *sorrow*. If teens are going to learn anything, they have to live with their bad decision. Love-and-logic parents know firsthand that *the best solution to any problem lives within the skin of the person who owns the problem.*

For example, Phil's seventeen-year-old daughter, Tiffany, comes home with alcohol on her breath. Should Phil talk to her about it immediately or in the morning? *Morning.* With anger or sadness? *Sadness.*

"Oh, I felt so sorry for you last night," Phil says the following morning. "I smelled alcohol on your breath. I'm starting to worry about you and alcohol. What would you guess about using the family car now?"

"I guess I might not get to use it," Tiffany replies.

"Good thinking," Phil replies.

Did Phil set a limit? Yes. Is Tiffany going to try to talk him out of it? Absolutely. Can she? No. Because no matter what Tiffany says, Phil can say, "Probably so."

"But I won't do it again," Tiffany begs.

"Probably so."

"Well, all the other kids get to do it."

"Probably so."

"Well," says Tiffany, trying to draw her father into an argument, "so you've got a big problem over alcohol, Dad, and now I can't drive and I've got to look like a dork at school because—"

"Probably so."

"Well," she persists, "how am I supposed to get to work at the jewelry shop?"

Now Tiffany's trying to give her problem to her dad.

If Phil gives her an answer, will she like it? No. It would be better for Phil to say, "I don't know. I was going to ask you the same thing."

"Well, I'll get fired!"

"Probably so."

Phil knows that if he gets angry with Tiffany, he will strip the consequences of her drinking of their power. By expressing anger he will insert himself into the process and impede the logic of the consequences from taking effect. By using "probably so" and keeping the focus on the effects of drinking and driving, Phil prevented Tiffany from focusing her anger on him. Instead, she was continually forced into facing the lesson taught by the consequences of her drinking.

Hurting from the Inside Out

Anger is an appealing emotion, especially when we're using it on our children. Punishment makes us feel so powerful. It makes us think we're in control. But as the children of drill sergeants will tell you, it doesn't work. When parents punish, they lose control over their teens. And the teens lose respect for their parents.

As a love-and-logic parent, Phil had learned to let Tiffany *hurt from the inside out*. He did this by allowing the natural consequences of her behavior to do the teaching. That way the consequence becomes the "bad guy" and Phil become the "good guy."

Allowing consequences while expressing empathy is one of the toughest parts of love-and-logic parenting. It takes effort to resist the desire to yell at your teenager when he comes home late without phoning you. And it takes effort to resist the temptation to rescue your daughter by chewing out the school officials when she doesn't make the cheerleading squad.

But if you can be truly sorry with teens and offer suggestions for ways they can put their lives back together, you will teach them the value of struggling through their problems in order to find solutions. You will also build a friendship with them while you prepare them for the responsibilities of dealing with the real world.

Children who grow in responsibility also grow in self-esteem—a prerequisite for achievement in the real world. As self-esteem and self-confidence grow, youngsters are better able to make it once the parental ties are cut.

The greatest gift we can give our youth is the knowledge that with God's help they can always look to themselves first for the answers to their problems. Teens who come at life with the attitude, "I can probably find my own solutions" become survivors. They have an edge in learning, relating to others, and making their way in the world.

LOVE-AND-LOGIC PRINCIPLE: BUILDING A LIFELONG RELATIONSHIP

Our stories about Tony and Tiffany illustrate the poignant pains and joys of growing up. They also provide a portrait of love-and-logic parents in action: parents who respect their children and guide them to live with the consequences of their actions.

The teens are still their children; the parents are still in authority. That relationship would exist whether the parents chose to be helicopters, drill sergeants, or consultants. But consultant love-and-logic parents are able to help their children learn how the real world operates.

Teens will gain confidence in themselves by making decisions and charting the courses for their own lives. You will notice that as they settle into their mid-twenties, their conversations turn to adult topics and their maturity level catches up with their physical size.

Love-and-logic parenting techniques aren't just to help you get through the rough spots of raising teenagers. They're tools to help you achieve the goal of guiding your youngster to live a responsible, productive, and happy life. By allowing your teen to achieve independence, you watch an adult blossom. And that adult, who happens to be your child, becomes your friend.

Living on the Edge

We hope we've encouraged you so far. But we don't want to give you the impression that parenting teenagers can be reduced to following a few easy steps. The steps are part of an overall process.

This process is primarily one of *change*. First, you're going through changes. After all, you've never parented teenagers before. Second, your teens are experiencing changes — both internally and externally — that you never could have imagined.

We'll be exploring those changes in part 2. They're a big part of what keeps parents of teenagers living on the edge. But with the basics of self-esteem, responsibility, sharing control, and expressing empathy while allowing consequences to do their work, you can confidently guide your son or daughter along the wild ride of adolescence. It doesn't have to be a white-knuckle trip — not all the time, anyway! Take heart and have fun.

NOTE
1. Sylvia B. Rimm, Ph.D., *How to Parent So Children Will Learn* (Watertown, WI: Apple Publishing Co., 1990).

PART II

❖

Living on the Edge:
The Wild and Wonderful
Challenges
of Parenting Teenagers

5

FASTEN YOUR SEAT BELT
AND ENJOY THE RIDE

❖

One of the most beneficial things that I (Jim) learned to say to my oldest child was, "Well, Susie, I've never been a parent of a fourteen-year-old before. So I'm probably going to make a lot of mistakes this year with you. I hope you'll help me through it. I'll try to help you through it."

Guess what I said when she was fifteen? "Well, Susie, I've never been a parent of a fifteen-year-old before. This is tough, isn't it? We have to go through it every year." She got to the point where she would empathize with me and say, "Dad, you're not doing that bad."

That kind of reassurance helped me ride out the storms of my children's adolescence. Perhaps you're riding out the storms yourself.

A hurricane of questions, doubts, and fears swirls around parents as their children approach adolescence. For parents whose children are already teens, it may feel that the hurricane has descended.

These questions and feelings are natural. And although it sounds like odd advice for a weathering a hurricane, the best thing you can do is to *get calm and relax*.

As we stated earlier, it's important for you to take good care of yourself. The feelings you have are real, the questions you have about your children are important. But stay calm.

How do you find calm in a storm? The first order of business is to organize your thoughts. We'll start with what's happening to you, then we'll deal with what kind of teen you have.

WHY PARENTS SHOULD RELAX

We're raising children, and we wonder how we're doing. For a lot of things we do in life, we receive some form of tangible recognition. In school, we get report cards. At work, we get performance evaluations or paychecks. But nobody gives us a report card in parenting. How our teens develop is really our only performance evaluation.

But that's a dicey proposition. One day it might tell us we're doing okay; the next day it might indicate we'd better hurry up and get some job training.

We wrestle internally with how our daughters and sons will turn out. What if they don't become model citizens? What does that say about us as parents? Guilt creeps in.

Maybe that's what makes us typical parents. We often feel guilty.

Have you spent time wondering how other people think of you because of the way your children behave? Your teen's out doing such-and-such and you don't have control. You feel guilty.

Guilt springs up from all sorts of nooks and crannies:

◆ Our teens' mood swings.
◆ Our teens don't talk to us as much as they used to.
◆ Our teens would rather be with their friends than home with us.
◆ Our teens tend to question or even reject our values.

Are we justified in feeling guilty about these things? No. These attitudes and behaviors are common for teenagers. That nagging thought, "If I were a better parent, my teen wouldn't be this way" is *normal*. Other parents are feeling the same way. That doesn't mean it's true.

Guilt isn't the only thing going on when we're parents of teenagers. We also have a sense of failure. And our offspring obligingly assist us in that. They keep a tally on where they think we're falling short: "My friend's dad owns a BMW," they'll say, with the not-too-subtle hint of "so when are you going to get with it?" They're quick to point out that all the other parents are doing a better job than we are.

But remember, "All of this shall pass, and they shall be teenagers no longer." And you'll notice that their attitudes will change, and your guilt will fade. As Mark Twain is quoted as saying, his parents got a lot smarter after his adolescence: "When I was a boy of fourteen, my father was so ignorant I could hardly stand to have the old man around. But when I got to be twenty-one, I was astonished at how much the old man had learned in seven years."

Why Worry?
A lot of people spend a lot of time worrying about what could go wrong. Remember, *worry is the price you pay in advance for most of the things in life that never happen.*

You only have so much time with your children, and you have two basic ways of looking at it. You can choose to spend that time thinking about all the things that could go wrong. Yup—plenty of opportunity there. Or, you can put that energy into thinking about how you can build a more positive relationship with your children. It's up to you.

Personally, we'd rather you made the second choice. And one place to start is learning to work with your children without criticizing or interrogating them.

Many parents over-analyze their parenting until they're afraid to open their mouths for fear they'll say the wrong thing to their teens. And sure — they often *do* say the wrong things. So what? That's not going to hurt the teenagers. That can get repaired along the way. It's a whole lot better to communicate *something* than to clam up because you're afraid it's going to come out wrong.

Relax. Don't let worry make you tongue-tied.

Listen and Learn

Getting close to your teen requires your effort to understand what he or she is experiencing. You can learn by listening to what your teen is telling you — but don't expect polite explanations.

Just as salmon are driven to swim upstream to spawn, so teenagers are driven to meet the awakening needs of independence and adulthood. But it's highly unlikely that a teen is going to sit you down to explain his or her needs: "Mom, Dad, let's talk about us. I'll be going through some pretty needy times during the next few years. You just have to understand that I'll need this, and I'll probably act like. . . ." This conversation will not take place. Your teen will show you what he or she needs by acting it out. And you can "listen" and learn.

Teens may try to meet their needs through foolish or even dangerous actions. As a result, parents feel threatened. We feel like we're doing a bad job. We feel guilty. We're failing — we'd better tighten control. We worry some more.

What do our teens feel when we clamp down on their actions? A stronger desire to show us how important those needs are. So they act out to communicate to us, "You will not control me. I will get my way." The teenager also feels a loss of love: "My needs are not being met, and Mom and Dad are doing everything they can to control me."

Then we feel a loss of control, and we, too, feel a loss of love. The relationships start to go downhill. It's a deteriorating cycle.

What should you do when your teen is acting out? Relax. Listen and learn. Don't worry. We often dig a grave that's pretty hard to get out of during these teenage years. Instead, maybe we can just back off a little, acknowledge those needs, and then say to our teen, "Yes, this is important. Let me help you grow through this. How can I help you accomplish things that are important to you?"

We're not talking about material things here. We're talking about giving our teen the chance to feel independent. We can say, "How can I help you do that so that you still take good care of yourself and I don't have to feel scared? Let's talk about that."

If we can get our teens to talk with us by saying to them, "Yes, I want you to get your needs met," do you think they might help us get *our* needs met? Maybe you could say, "You know, as a parent, I have needs, too. I need to feel like I'm doing a good job. I need to feel like I'm getting you ready for the real world. I need to feel like I've been doing the job in such a way that you'll take good care of yourself and will continue to be a happy person as you go through life."

Parents and teens need to talk to each other about their needs. It's okay for us to say, "Here's what I'm trying to do. Am I doing something that's getting in your way of you? Am I hurting you in some way? Tell me about it. What's the pouting all about? Can you put it into words? What are these tears telling me? What is the anger and the stomping around really trying to tell me?"

In other words, we're taking our teen's actions seriously as often as possible and saying, "Can you put that in words for me so I'll really understand it, and I won't misread it?" With this style of communication, you'll find that many of your parenting worries simply melt away. Once your teen does put feelings into words, never try to straighten out his or her thoughts. You will get much better results by saying, "Thanks for sharing that!"

SOME THINGS PARENTS NEED TO UNDERSTAND

Parents who have learned to ask their teens questions and get them to think have faced the issue of what lies ahead: "My thirteen-year-old is going to be out in the world in five years, assuming that she doesn't run away from home first. How can I start operating this home the way the real world operates?"

These parents have also come to grips with what happens to their children during the teenage years:

Changing thoughts. When children are elementary school age, they usually want to tell us everything—who did what, who said what to whom, what they think about all of it.

Then when children move into adolescence, they start having a lot of thoughts like, "Gee, I wonder if my mother can handle what I'm thinking—maybe I shouldn't tell her." They have a lot of thoughts they can't articulate.

Changing values. There are a lot of things adolescents would rather not share with us because it might be different from our value system.

Changing sexuality. Teens aren't going to whip hummers on their parents like, "Hey, Mom, let me tell you why my showers are so long." Their bodies develop, their hormones kick into gear, and they find themselves experiencing sexuality for the first time—and none of those changes is conducive to open discussion with Mom or Dad.

Changing appearance. Youngsters get extremely sensitive in early adolescence—ages twelve to thirteen—because they're not quite sure what's right or what's wrong in appearance, what to do with their fantasies about the other sex, and whether or not that zit is the only thing that shows on their face.

Parents who can interact well with their teens also know that birth order typically affects how their children will behave and act on their needs:

1. The firstborn is basically Einstein—the thinker, the doer, the doctor, the lawyer.

2. The middle children tend to be Picassos, because they look in on themselves and become sensitive.

3. The youngest child is the talk-show host. By the time that last one comes along, we're pretty relaxed as parents. We allow natural consequences to fall, and we give the child a lot of love. We're not quite as uptight, so he or she has the freedom to say, "Hey, world, here I am!"

All teenagers possess these common traits. But the common traits will work themselves out in different ways, depending on what kind of teen you have.

THREE TYPES OF TEENS

Five-year-olds may have tremendous similarities in their parenting needs. But as they get older, their paths diverge. We've observed three types of adolescents:

Early bloomers. The first type describes those children who get along well in the first and second years of life. By the time they reach the sixth grade, they're good kids. They turn out well, regardless of how rebellious they may have seemed during adolescence.

These children move along smoothly for several reasons. First, their mothers didn't abuse drugs during pregnancy. Second, their parents provided love and nurturing for them during the first twelve months. Third, their parents applied wise and loving discipline in the second year of life, saying "no" and meaning it when the child's behavior was inappropriate.

Late bloomers. The second type of teenagers had problems in their first and second years, but by age eleven they have their acts together and make it all right through adolescence — and probably through life.

Troubled teens. This third type describes children who had problems originating in their first and second years that continued through age eleven and beyond. They don't get along well with parents or peers. They play the role of victim all the time, charming and conning people easily, hoarding or gorging on food. These children often become delinquents.

The foundations of personality are laid in the first two years of life. Children are predisposed to difficulties during adolescence when, in their early years, they have:

◆ Pain that the parents can't relieve.
◆ Genetic predispositions that the parents can't alleviate.
◆ Early abuse and neglect.
◆ The possible use of drugs and/or alcohol by the parents.

These predispositions are more pronounced in some children than in others. Their genetic makeup can determine how well they will be able to handle environmental factors such as neglect or abuse. And the way they cope with adolescence can also depend on the ability of their parents to discover proper parenting techniques.

Some of those predispositions will not easily be relieved by the techniques outlined in this book. If a child had fetal alcohol syndrome, for example, no amount of love-and-logic parenting will bring about an easy adolescence. Nor will parenting techniques erase problems such as developmental defects and abnormalities resulting from certain congenital illnesses. The child will inevitably "feel different" from other kids during the latency years between three and eleven. If you suspect your child has experienced such predispositions, we strongly urge you to seek competent professional help.

Because personality is shaped so early in life, parenting is a lot easier when the foundation is correctly laid. Many parents of nineteen-year-olds will ask, "What can I do for this kid?" Not a whole lot, really, except give them something to read on personal development. At nineteen, a child is now in the adult world. The patterns he's developed through his adolescence are firmly set, and he's achieved independence — for better or for worse — from his parents.

But parents can and still do have an influence on their fifteen-year-olds. They can use their influence in the home to help their youngsters learn how to make choices and live with the consequences.

Now let's take a closer look at the three types of adolescents we identified above.

Early Bloomers

The majority of teens fall into the first category of those who were well-adjusted from birth through age eleven: the early bloomers. If parents got along well with their children through sixth grade or age eleven, it doesn't matter how bad adolescence goes — even if they act rebellious as teens. Everything will tend to work out all right in the long run.

Of course, tragic behavior such as heavy drug use or promiscuity can threaten adolescent development and parents' relationships to their teens. But barring those extreme conditions, if their parents have enjoyed good relations with their children through age eleven, they can relax.

Sure, there are teens who don't want to talk about things because they're too ashamed and too uncertain and too thrown off-balance. Others are very lucky teens. They have a very high self-image and have had very good communication with their parents all along. They will go through periods of withdrawal and questioning because body, mind, and emotions are changing faster in adolescence than at any other time in life. But these are normal issues, and the teens will turn out fine.

For example, even normal, well-adjusted children verbally snipe at their parents. It's common for eleven-year-old boys to be angry and for thirteen-year-old girls to get irritated and make nasty comments. That's part of the natural processes of growing up. Part of it is hormonal. Part of it is the teen's apprehension over realizing that in a few years he or she may have a job or a new name. These are profound changes, and often teens' only response to such anxiety is to lash out verbally at their parents. Under such stressful conditions, adults do the same thing.

In response to this behavior, parents can say to their teens, "I know you're angry—that happens to kids and adults, too. But it's an irritation to be around you, so why don't you have dinner in your room?"

Late Bloomers

Then there are teens who had difficulties in the first and second years of life, such as undiagnosed health problems, but otherwise experienced a relatively well-adjusted childhood. These late bloomers will have few serious problems during adolescence. Early problems can crop up again, however, in several ways.

Those problems often revolve around early developmental issues over health, appearance, and social adjustment. But they're overcome by *understanding the causes of the problems, not excusing wrong behavior.*

Fred was an ugly kid. Not only was he gawky like a lot of youngsters, he was severely nearsighted from birth. He couldn't play catch because he never developed eye-hand coordination, and he had trouble with his schoolwork because he couldn't see the chalkboard. His teachers and parents gradually found out about his vision difficulties and were able to correct most of it with glasses.

Now Fred is thirteen. He's learned to apply himself to

his studies, but he sometimes exhibits antisocial behavior from the years of taunts with catcalls of "four-eyes" and other insults.

Fred's parents waited until they were in a good mood to talk about Fred's difficulties with him.

"We know you're mad a lot," they opened.

"Yeah," Fred responded, and looked down at the floor.

"How much of the time do you think others have it better?" they gently asked.

"Other kids *always* have it better," Fred hissed. "They can see without any stupid glasses."

"Well, to tell the truth, Fred, when you were little, other children *did* have it better," they agreed. "When other kids were playing catch, you couldn't see the ball; when others were making friends, you couldn't see them from across the classroom. Pal, we really understand that. If we grew up with those problems, we'd probably be feeling that, too."

"Yeah, well, I don't know what to say," Fred went on. "It's all so unfair."

Then Fred's parents turned the conversation to a new angle. "However, those who have an early handicap are given an equally large opportunity; because when they get over that handicap, they become more thoughtful, more understanding, and more aware than the people who never had that problem in the first place. Some of our greatest leaders were those who had to overcome difficult times."

"Yeah, but it's still not easy," Fred replied.

"We understand, and we do love you very much and want you to succeed."

Parents of late bloomers should level with their teens and tell them why they may be having problems in the family or society. But past or even lingering problems such as these are not excuses for antisocial behavior. Parents should offer explanations as ways of *understanding* the behavior. Teens need to grasp this reality: "My background means I have to work especially hard."

Teens with early childhood struggles should be given the expectation that they can overcome those early things, and that their parents really appreciate their efforts. For example, when a child with early coordination problems makes the soccer team, it means they did extra work. Parents can also encourage their teens to make friends despite their earlier problems.

With this kind of parenting, late bloomers learn to own their own triumphs and failures. Parents should neither overprotect teens nor aggravate their problems by excusing outbursts of anger or other manifestations of earlier developmental problems.

The same techniques can be applied to troubled teens. For example, parents can say, "Sweetheart, you were abused by your grandfather when you were a child. That was awful, we understand your pain. That's why you're angry. So you're going to have to work on it." The background is a reason without being an excuse. It is understood, not excused, on the basis of background or the problem.

This brings up another parenting approach for teens struggling to overcome early difficulties: *toleration without permission*. Don't ever say, "Oh, now that I understand it, I excuse it." Give your child a background for understanding why he or she may be having difficulties. But regardless of cause, do not tolerate antisocial and especially criminal activity. Teens often imply by their words and actions, "You *are* going to tolerate this" while using their past to justify it.

Let your teen know you're empathetic with his or her difficulties. But make it clear from the outset that you won't tolerate inappropriate behavior. And then act on your convictions. If you warn your teen not to throw rocks at houses, don't excuse the deed when the neighbors call up to complain about broken windows.

For a geopolitical analogy, European leaders constantly warned Adolf Hitler in the 1930s to curb his expansionist policies. But after Hitler seized Czechoslovakia, they said, "Well, all right; but don't do it again."

Sometimes a teen's early developmental problems were unintentionally caused by the parents themselves.

Lisa, for example, was allergic to milk. But her parents didn't know it, and they constantly scolded her for crying, especially after feeding her. Lisa and her parents didn't find out that she had this allergy until she was fourteen.

How should her parents respond now? "We're sorry that it happened, and at the time we were doing the best we knew how." Parents don't need to ask for forgiveness for their earlier well-intentioned actions. They should just state the facts of what happened and express their genuine regret. Teens can use a request for forgiveness to validate their resentment. It also opens them to the idea that they just might *not* forgive it.

If your teen seems to resent you, don't say, "Boy this resentment hurts me." If you do, the young teen is going to respond, "Good, Mom and Dad deserve to hurt."

The better response, and the one that will help build trust, is, "If you go through life resenting me, it's going to eat you from the inside out. I hope you won't hang on to resentment, because it's going to hurt you."

For teens who had problems in the first year of life, a little bit of trust can go a long way. Over time that trust will build, just the way a pearl forms over a grain of sand.

One way to build on that trust is to ask for more eye contact. Say, "It looks like you're having trouble with eye contact. I hope you get over it." Or, "I'd appreciate it if you looked me in the eye; I'd appreciate it if you'd lower your voice."

Again, the point here is that *parents are telling their children what they want instead of telling their children what to do.* We're almost always on shaky ground when we try to order our children, such as, "Look at me when I'm talking to you." When we try to force our children to maintain eye contact with us, their eyes will focus on an object behind us, therefore ignoring us.

But there are some disturbed teens who don't have even a grain of trust to build on. This happens if your teen had first-year-of-life difficulties and never developed basic trust. Such children grow through toddlerhood with extreme control problems that continue through elementary school. Those kids are control problems for everyone in the environment — parents and teachers.

Such children, to be reached, generally need a very highly structured situation that forces them to conform. This leads the teen to explode in anger and rage. The rage and anger are accepted by the authority figures, and this acceptance leads to trust. Thus, seemingly harsh environments can build a great deal of trust, especially when the *process* is completed. This is the reason that some states work with delinquent teenagers in "boot camp" settings.

Troubled Teens

Almost all children who suffer chronic problems from birth through age eleven are going to have significant problems in adolescence, and parents are going to be caught in the storm. Perhaps the parents didn't cause the problems, but they will certainly have to live with them. These troubled teens are still a minority group, but their numbers are rising.

Disturbed teenagers have blocked in a great deal of rage, which smolders in some of the following manifestations:

- They don't like to be touched.
- They avoid eye contact.
- They don't want people to give them relief.
- They have no trust.
- They have learning and food problems.

These teens probably will need professional help, and parents should not be embarrassed to seek it. Here are three ways parents can find out whether they have a troubled teen:

The best way is to *get a professional opinion* from a child psychologist or child psychiatrist. Be sure to find somebody who's very busy. That way, you screen out professionals who may simply be trying to hustle more clients to support themselves. Remember that credentials are no guarantee of a quality professional opinion.

Second, *ask for an outside perspective from someone with good teens.* Don't compare notes with someone who has similar problems. Church and school self-help parenting groups can be helpful here. Parents can find out through friends or parenting groups whether or not their problem is a normal part of adolescence or a serious situation requiring professional resources.

The third and least reliable way is to *rely on your own intuition.*

Don't assume your teen is disturbed just because he or she does things you don't like. That's a meaningless indicator. *All* children do things we don't like. The key question is this: "Are the things my teen is doing likely to be destructive to his or her life?"

"Destructive" does not always mean something that will eventually be harmful to teens. Outwardly destructive behavior can actually be constructive because teens are learning something about their lives. Just because teens get hurt doesn't mean all aspects of wrong behavior are ultimately bad. For example, running away from home could in part be beneficial, because the teen could learn some valuable lessons about life.

"Destructive" generally *does* mean something that teens do that will not teach them a lesson and enable them to benefit from the hurt. "Destructive" also can mean that the lifelong lesson of the pain of an action will outweigh the value of the learning experience. For example, if your son gets a girl pregnant and chooses not to marry her, the pain of child-support payments will last at least eighteen years, overriding any lessons he would learn from the consequences of irresponsible sexual behavior.

But parents should not protect their teens from reality. In a few years, they will be incapable of protecting their teens. The adult world is more harshly consequential than what most parents lay down to a teenager. And parents provide a loving context: "I'll let you experience the consequences of this because I love you." The adult world is either antagonistic or indifferent.

Parents of troubled teens can respond best by realizing that they must first take care of themselves and protect the rest of the family. A wise parent will say, "I can expect that John is going to have problems. I've got to make sure that the family and other kids are safe. I can't burden myself with guilt, and I can't burden my family with continued hardship. I can't burden the family with bills, because we could liquidate our estate with psychiatric or legal bills."

These parents can also reasonably lower their expectations because that's the reality of the situation. Reasonable expectations can reduce hurt and avoid paralysis from shock or surprise when something happens. Parents who stay away from hand-wringing are freed up to be more effective in their responses.

What youngsters in this situation need most desperately before they finally leave the home is to be around a healthy role model who can show them how to live a healthy, balanced life once they're on their own.

Often, however, parents rant and rave and threaten and accuse, which is just the opposite of taking care of themselves. When teens leave home and turn their backs on ranting parents, they've lost their last chance to figure out how to take care of themselves. Once they get out in the world, the odds are that they will take the lead of the modeling they saw in their parents. They'll go through life accusing and blaming everybody else and trying to control other people, instead of first taking care of themselves.

In most cases, parents who do a great job of taking care of themselves feel horrible and guilty and selfish when in fact they're doing the best thing possible. Paradoxically, *taking care of ourselves first* is what gives teens the possibility of getting better themselves.

If the family members allow themselves to suffer from John's behavior in order to make it easier on John, they become *enablers* for John's destructive behavior. John will think, "If I'm hard on my brothers and sisters, my parents will take care of me. If I'm in trouble with the law, my parents will bail me out."

In this context, helping becomes hurting. Helping becomes excusing. If you want to see people ravaged by such "helping," look at those who are dependent on long-term government subsidies. Look at those whose parents "helped" their children well into adulthood. When people are given a free ride, they never learn to start their engines. As a result, they become emotionally crippled, except under extraordinary circumstances.

When teens don't respond to the natural consequences of their wrong behavior, they might need to enter a day treatment program or move in with a relative.

However, when parents send a teen to live with relatives or in a detention home, they have to compare the resentment of a forced change of residence with the positive benefits that might occur. The teen probably will resent it. The more a teen can buy into such a decision by having a say-so in it, the better.

But there can come a time when a parent might simply say, "Kid, you have to go." This may occur when parents feel that the situation is intolerable for themselves and the rest of the family. At this point, they need an outside opinion on the legality of such a decision.

Incorrigible fifteen-year-olds will be incorrigible at home or on the street. They might as well be incorrigible on the street so they can be locked up in a structured environment. It sounds extremely harsh, but if the rest of the family is at risk it's a tough but necessary decision.

AGAIN, RELAX

Sometimes we forget that *we* went through periods in which we didn't communicate with *our* parents. When our teen starts to withdraw or experience difficulties, we may automatically assume that we've done something wrong. Or we may think back to what *we* were like at their age, and then jump all over them in fear of what they're up to.

Because we don't get report cards or other feedback, it's typical for us to worry that things are going wrong. "The kid isn't talking to me: I've got to do something better!" But most times it's just a normal phase our teen is going through.

Some phases are tougher than others, especially if a teen's behavior threatens the safety of the rest of the family. But most times, we stand a good chance that things will work out all right if we remember that we are the parents, that we're in charge, that we must take good care of ourselves first, and that our goal is to help our children grow up to be responsible adults.

We'll make it; they'll make it. We could call these years of raising teenagers "Goof and Grow." We learn the hard way, don't we? We make a lot of mistakes. But the end result, a responsible teenager about to become a responsible adult, is worth it.

6

UNDERSTANDING TEENS FROM THE INSIDE OUT:
Internal Changes in Adolescence

❖

Fourteen-year-old Joni came into my (Foster's) office, sobbing.

"When I was a little girl, Dr. Cline, my parents didn't have to know where I was every minute. They didn't have to know who my friends were or if I was late for dinner," she told me.

"But now I'm fourteen. I grew up and they pick on me because I'm not a little girl anymore and I look like a woman. It's not my fault that I grew boobs."

It's normal — and regrettable — that when the girl curves out, the parents clamp down. Boys, too, experience similar clamp-downs from their parents.

The rapid physical, cognitive, and psychological changes that adolescents undergo can frighten parents who have forgotten that they survived those very same changes. These children are literally becoming adults. Yet as parents grow out of parenting children into parenting teenagers, they often react like Joni's mom and dad did: they unwittingly impose more rules when their kids don't look like children anymore. Teens are not children, and the way they're treated should change accordingly.

We must not minimize what happens in our youngsters' bodies and minds, nor should we dismiss those changes by telling our kids they're "just going through a phase" or "just looking for an excuse to rebel." Teens themselves don't know what's happening and often can't explain what it feels like. They're like big fish outgrowing a small aquarium.

In a sense, adolescence is the toddler stage of adulthood. Toddlers can go through ups and downs as they experience rapid changes in their physical and verbal dexterity. For the first time in their lives, toddlers are learning that they can be independent in their own little ways, and they will ride their new freedom for all it's worth until Mom or Dad says "no" in order to protect them.

In adolescence, children go through another phase of growth and independence. But now, the consequences of children's independence are a lot more intense. How parents deal with their children's adolescence depends in part upon the way they handled their children's earlier years. If teenagers didn't establish their identities in healthy ways when they were younger, they may push their needs for independence that much further. In other words, they have to take more risks, more chances, be more bizarre, and act out in ways that communicate, in essence, "I am not my parent." Those actions are often perceived as "rebellion."

If parents have brought up their children to see themselves as individual persons—not just so-and-so's child—most likely the adolescent identity crisis will not be as intense nor the rebellion as deep.

Most of what we call rebellion is a natural outgrowth of a series of profound changes in a teen. Those changes — the greatest changes a person experiences in his or her life — include radical shifts in mind, body, and personal values. They are wonderful and weird all at once. The more you understand them, the better a parent — and friend — you can be to your teen.

That's why we're going to devote this chapter to understanding teens from the inside out. We'll look at the primary internal changes in the areas of cognitive thinking, physical development and sexuality, psychological development and values formation, and self-expression (adolescent rebellion).

CHANGES IN THINKING

Don't be surprised if your thirteen-year-old replaces her play-by-play descriptions of her day with sudden, angry outbursts. What's happening is a gradual, almost magical shift in the way your child thinks. Up until the early teens, a child thinks immaturely with little ability to conceptualize.

Jean Piaget, the famous Swiss psychologist, closely studied the development of thinking in children. He referred to the thinking of elementary and early junior high schoolers as "concrete operations" and named mature thinking "formal operations." Piaget found that mature thinking arises out of the natural transitional stages in growing up and can be neither hurried nor delayed by parents or educational structures.

Preadolescent children are very "concrete" in their thinking. They follow the rules. They do what their parents say. They think in terms of the specific, or concrete, objects in their world. Later, when they reach the developmental stage in which they can think abstractly, they can make judgments such as, "Well, in this situation, this makes sense."

For instance, let's say that seventeen-year-old Frank is required by his parents to be home by 10:00 p.m. But at 9:50 p.m., Frank is thinking, "It's getting late, but John's out of gas and needs a lift home. It'll take me a half-hour. I'll be home late, but circumstances require it." A fifth-grader, however, would cling to, "My parents said be home by five. No matter what, I have to get home at five."

During the first eleven years of life, the mind is in a very concrete mode, which is necessary for our very survival. We learn to follow Mom around and do what Mom tells us. Why? Because human beings are born nine months premature. They can't get up and move around right away when they're born. All other mammal babies start swimming or walking shortly after birth. But not human babies: in their first nine months, their heads and brains are still developing. They're not doing much thinking for themselves. They're heavily reliant on their parents to do their thinking for them.

During this time it's very easy for us to tell the child in the drill sergeant way, "Do this, do that. Do it my way." Or we might take the helicopter approach: "Oh, honey, don't worry. We'll take care of you."

Children change as their modes of thinking change. About the time Tommy reaches twelve or thirteen, his brain switches over to abstract thinking. Now he can start making conceptual connections that he couldn't make earlier. For example, think of how strange and funny little children's jokes are. The things they laugh at—bald slapstick is a knee-slapper every time—are very concrete. They miss our humor when we try to joke with them. But when they become teenagers, they can be a lot of fun: they can participate in our jokes.

But it isn't much fun when little Tommy turns into big Tommy with a shaved head, a pierced ear, and a snarl on his lips. He may not want to participate in the *family*, never mind our jokes. But Tommy has no control over these changes, just as he has no control over his developing fertility and the level of testosterone in his body, the hormone that will give him his secondary sex characteristics. Tommy's sister Annie isn't much different. She, too, will go through changes in thinking and behavior leading up to her body's trigger of the hormone estrogen, producing her secondary sex characteristics.

New Ways of Relating

As children transition into formal operational thinking after age eleven and begin to question their parents' behavior, they often display their new thinking style through anger, outbursts, and stinging retorts.

For the first time, they can truly judge their own ability to handle difficult situations — and for the first time, their judgment on issues affecting their lives may be better than that of their parents! *This new ability to think is at the heart of many parent-child misunderstandings.*

Here are some of the changes you may notice as a result of your teen's newly mature thinking:

1. You will be less likely to hear long and detail-packed stories of movies, friends, school, or other activities.
2. For the first time, your child understands the meaning of parables and sayings such as, "People who live in glass houses shouldn't throw stones."
3. Your teen will begin to appreciate political cartoons for more than just a character's big nose or funny appearance.
4. You will no longer hear questions that seem to have such obvious answers. The phrase "I don't get it, Mom" will fade away.
5. Your youngster will begin to question, for the first time, whether or not the end justifies the means.

6. Your children will no longer buy into your value system automatically just because they love you.
7. Your teen will begin to question and comment on parental behavior from a more objective perspective.

Let Them Take Flight!
Although parents may find some of these changes confusing, and at times disruptive, it helps to understand that they are a natural and important part of a child's development. You can expect this shift toward conceptual adult thinking to take place over a period of about six months, for most children during age eleven to twelve.

Parents who have raised responsible children can welcome these changes as a major step in their child's development into adulthood. They can also recognize it as a time to back off, let their children unfold their newly found cerebral wings, and take flight. They'll be equipped to leave the nest when it's time.

Another amazing thing is that just about the time the brain switches over to abstract thinking, children are also given the power to reproduce. In other words, the Creator—with utmost wisdom—created humans so that they would not be able to procreate before they could think maturely.

PHYSICAL CHANGES

Scientists don't know yet exactly what causes these changes in thinking and in the body during adolescence. The changes might be triggered by a cause-and-effect relationship of brain on body or vice versa. They may be a part of the natural unfolding of DNA, the genetic material supplying the building blocks of life.

We know that other physical changes can affect emotions and thinking. As soon as hormones fluctuate, so do thoughts and emotions. For example, women experience postpartum depression; men often experience anger and depression after a coronary attack.

Changes in teens' ability to think may relate to these other physical and emotional shifts. As children develop physically, they can step out of their environment and look at it in a more conceptual and rational way. They can put words on it: "My mom worries too much" or "My mom is overprotective." A younger child couldn't articulate that except in a vague way.

Many physical changes are common to both girls and boys. These range from growing bigger in size to changing preferences for a variety of foods. It's also normal for teens to like loud music with a pronounced beat.

But the changes that make parents the most nervous are clustered around issues of sexuality and gender identity.

Changes in Girls

Joni, the girl we mentioned earlier who resented her parents clamping down as she matured physically, found out firsthand that girls develop earlier than boys. So parents naturally get concerned about girls earlier than about boys.

Most girls start menstruating around age nine or ten. Parents can take development in stride as they discuss it with their daughters. The best way to handle it is by asking questions: "Brenda, how much do you know about menstruation? What do you know about your first period?"

Questions are far better than lectures. Otherwise, your daughter—who probably has learned an immense amount about sex on the street—goes to her friends, rolls her eyes, and tells them, "Can you believe it? My mom told me about the birds and the bees!"

If Mom isn't around, Dad can discuss it with the daughter. It's best, though, to have a female confidante.

Girls start wearing bras at about age ten or eleven. They

should be allowed to decide what kind of bras they want. Their mothers, in turn, should be excited for them and shop with their daughters. It's best to take the attitude, "Isn't this neat," instead of approaching bra shopping with apprehension.

Even though the girl is filling out, she still needs hugs from Dad and Mom. She still needs the touching and roughhousing that the family has done in the past. The interpersonal relationships between daughter and parents should continue to develop as she develops physically.

Regrettably, fathers sometimes feel nervous and quit touching their daughters. Girls may interpret this hesitancy as rejection, reacting in ways their fathers don't know how to handle. A cycle ensues as the daughter's apprehension fuels her father's apprehension, and so on.

Changes in Boys
Boys don't develop as early as girls. Male hormones kick in a little later than female hormones.

Parents should be able to discuss sexuality with their sons matter-of-factly, just as with their daughters. And again, using a line of questioning is the most effective approach. Adolescent boys, in most cases more so than adolescent girls, have picked up a library of knowledge about sex on the street. Parents shouldn't assume that their teens know it all, or know it correctly. So instead of telling them about erections, Mom and Dad should ask them what they know about them.

Parents should also be excited about shopping for jock straps with their sons. As with their daughters, they should convey to their sons, "Isn't this neat?" when shopping for such personal items.

As boys develop physically, the fathers may subconsciously feel threatened: there's another young buck in the herd. They might be resentful of Mom hugging the boy. It's usually a low-grade, back-of-the-mind kind of irritation. So Dad responds by being more distant or more controlling. And the boy reacts by rebelling and being more demanding in return.

The other problem is that Dad may not give the boy the hugs, the arm around the shoulder, the fun stuff that went on when the son was eight. But even at thirteen, the son is still a little boy inside. His need for affection from *both* parents hasn't let up.

TEACHING YOUTHS ABOUT SEX

There's more than one "right way" to teach your teens about sex and growing up, as long as your son or daughter feels listened to and taken seriously.

As a parent it is important for you to clearly express your own religious and moral values on sexuality. To stay silent is to rob your child of the wisdom you have accumulated.

As an example, the instruction related to sexual behavior in the Bible has stood the test of time. In a day when an increasing number of young teens are reaping the serious emotional consequences of premature sexual activity, out of wedlock pregnancies, and AIDS and other sexually transmitted diseases, the Scriptures' advice to save sex for marriage is extremely relevant, "safe," and effective.

Parents need to emphasize with their children the seriousness of sex in its nature and consequences. Our language reflects how we take this beautiful, loving gift and turn it upside down—"making love" turns into language reflecting being hurt, such as "screwed over."

You can joke about sex as long as it's clear that you're taking the subject and your teens seriously. That's okay; humor can relieve tension. We also joke about nuclear war, but we know it's serious.

Most important is maintaining open communication,

so teens don't withdraw from talking about things that are troubling them. If you don't know the answer to a question, tell your child you'll find the answer.

Part of the difficulty in teaching teens about sex occurs when parents project their own thoughts and values onto their children. Some adults think to themselves, *If I were young again and knew then what I know now, I might have sex.* Then they unfairly assume that their children are out looking for opportunities.

Give teens some room to grow on their own while letting them know that you expect them to be responsible. Instead of giving them the impression that you think they're on the prowl for sex, communicate to them the assumption that they are morally responsible and will live up to your expectations.

Despite what you might think from pop culture, most teens aren't going to rush out and have sex. Responsible teens are still reticent to have sex early.

Have you ever wondered how much of the considerable sexual activity among high school students is fueled through subtle encouragement from adults? Teen sex appears to have become a self-fulfilling prophecy. Society assumes that teens have sex, so they do have sex — and then society says, "Oh no."

Many teens feel resentful about all the talk about sex, saying, "Why are they talking to me about contraceptives? I don't want to have sex." This kind of emphasis tends to shove teens into it. The messages we send on this topic must not only be sensitive but clear.

Sex and Teenage Rebellion

Some teens who harbor chronic resentment toward parents will use sex as a means of rebellion. As their resentment becomes self-destructive, they may think they can vent that resentment through inappropriate sexual activity, tacky friends, and delinquent behavior. Some daughters try to get back at their mothers by getting pregnant, especially if they have been raised in extremely rigid, religious homes. They may go out of their way to find boys who grew up in homes with a different value system. When something like that happens, it's often rebellion.

To thwart rebellious sexual behavior, parents can make it clear to their teens that they mess *themselves* up when they engage in such activity.

Dads should have a discussion with their sons (without implying that their teens are going to have sex) that is sensitive and to the point. In addition to addressing the rights and wrongs of premarital sexual behavior, Dad should make clear that in this day and age, it's legally dangerous for a boy to have sex with a girl. If the girl gets pregnant, wants to keep the baby, and marriage for whatever reason is not an option, the legal cards are stacked against the boy (no matter what assurances the girl might have given him about what birth control she was using). He's legally and financially responsible for his child through college. If the girl ends up feeling rejected or is controlling or angry, she can make the boy's life miserable for the next seventeen years.

Another major risk of promiscuous behavior comes from sexually transmitted diseases (STDs). There is an astronomical multiplication factor for people who engage in promiscuous sex. When individuals have sex with another person, they virtually have sex with every person their partner had sex with, and with all the people *those* partners had sex with, and on and on. The risks for diseases such as AIDS, gonorrhea, syphilis, and chlamydia multiply with frequent sexual behavior. STDs have a history of decimating entire cultures.

Male/Female Differences in How Teens View Sex

Guys and girls look at sex in different ways. A girl usually regards sex as being closely related to reproduction. A guy usually considers sex a physical and emotional release.

Both guys and girls should understand that they'll feel guilty when they have sex—although girls tend to experience the consequences more intensely than boys. The emotional consequences include not only the risk of getting dumped by the other person but also the possibility that early sexual activity can dull the pleasure and bonding of sex in marriage.

Sexual Orientation

Although this book assumes that heterosexuality is preferable to homosexuality, our purpose here is not to address the moral implications of orientation, but to focus on the parent-teen relationship once it becomes an issue. Parents are increasingly having to face the issue of sexual orientation, and sweeping it under the rug is not helpful. This book is about open communication. Not to bring it up means that we aren't open and we're being hypocritical. Our impression is that when teens move toward a homosexual issue, it should not be considered rebellion.

Obviously, it's okay to express the desire and hope to our children that they will live a heterosexual life. But if they have a homosexual orientation, we must love them just as much. Christ's message in the New Testament is very clear: God's children are all and equally loved. And just because we accept the lifestyle of our children doesn't necessarily mean we approve of it.

Although after much research the root causes of homosexuality are still unclear and certainly complex, one way parents can help guide their teens to heterosexuality is by continuing the physical contact they extended when the kids were younger. The key is touch. Dads should be physically loving toward sons, just as moms should be physically loving toward their daughters. Gender identity problems have been suspected to occur when moms are overly touchy with sons while dads are distant. The same holds true when dads are overly touchy with their daughters while moms are distant.

If your teen has a homosexual orientation, however, it doesn't mean you have done anything wrong. Some parents think it's a negative reflection on them. These parents face a growth experience. They have to sort through their feelings to figure out how much is guilt, sorrow, fear, and anger.

Homosexuality may be the ultimate test for many parents of whether they can separate out acceptance of their children from approval of their behavior and lifestyle. We can accept a troubling reality and still wish it were different. It is essential for our children to know that we love them no less.

PSYCHOLOGICAL CHANGES (CHANGES IN VALUES)

Teens say the darndest things. Sometimes they say *outrageous* things such as, "I don't want to go to your church anymore because I've decided to become a satanist."

Why do they do that? Here are four big reasons:

They want to hear what's right. They want their parents to respond and give them the right perspective, and so they try to provoke the correct information.

They want interaction and attention. If teens are hungering for some emotion and reasonable comments don't elicit a response, they'll try a different tack. When parents don't express joy and excitement over the right things, teens will seek negative reaction over the wrong things. An apathetic reaction is as bad as an inflexible reaction.

They want to make the parent become upset and feel pain because the parent-child relation isn't good. When teens are in pain, they want their parents to recognize it and feel it too. An outrageous comment can give them the momentary satisfaction they're looking for: "*Yes,* I got a response; I got my parent to hurt."

They're using the conversation to get control. Shocking declarations get parents' attention — reluctantly. Suddenly, the teen is initiating and the parent is reacting. In that moment, the teen is in control; the parent isn't. This gives the teen a feeling of power.

These encounters are evidence of the psychological ferment in the adolescent psyche. As children turn into teenagers, their mental tumblers are falling into place. They can make observations about parents that reveal sharpening psychological insight, such as, "Dad, it's hard for you to let go of little things."

Teens are increasingly able to articulate these observations, but not diplomatically. They might make an insightful remark to parents but in a harsh manner.

Parents defeat themselves when they try to thwart their teen's psychological development by saying, "Don't ever say that again." Every time "shut up" is expressed, it's a shut-down of communication, which undermines parental authority.

Basically, teens' psychological development is what happens when their new brainpower interacts with their old values. Coping with this clash of realities takes time and patience on everybody's part. Good communication skills don't unfold in the DNA. But they can be learned.

We're always on safe ground when we present our thoughts in a non-threatening manner: "This is the way I feel, and I hope you think. . . ." Generally, we're on dangerous ground whenever we tell others how to think, how to feel, or what to do.

Let's say Heather comes home from school and tells Mom, "I want to be like the Buddhists, so I'm not going to eat meat anymore."

A typical drill sergeant response to such a comment would be, "Nonsense! I don't want you hanging around those weirdos at school. Now sit down and eat your dinner." And a typical helicopter response would be, "Oh, honey!

Isn't our religion good enough for you?"

In this case, Mom just spent two hours on a mouth-watering prime rib dinner. Mom should concentrate on her own tastes and desires and say, "Well, that's more beef for Dad and me. I hope it works out for you and us." (After all, Heather could be absolutely right about the vegetarian diet!) Once again, from the parental point of view, *acceptance does not mean approval.* The family does not have to make the change with Heather. Mom doesn't go out of her way to cook tofu and soybeans, nor does the rest of the family avoid such foods — that would put Heather in negative control of the family. If, in a case like this, you can make everybody happy and cook vegetarian, then great.

When Values Become Self-Destructive

Not all teen psychological development issues involve outrageous comments or flirtations with values that are in one week and out the next. Some choices in values are destructive and can threaten a teen's personality or slow down his or her development for a number of years.

For example, Todd wanted to join a rigid authoritarian religious sect. The sect was known for financially fleecing its members and splitting young people from their families. So Todd's parents sent him to live with his grandparents for a while. Todd was a fairly healthy child who wanted to do something unhealthy, so the parents got him out of the environment.

If we feel our teens are going to do something that will mess up their life for a long time to come, then it's our responsibility to protect them. But that responsibility carries an inherent danger: if we're not careful, our fears could override our judgment in making this sort of decision.

Parents must weigh the possible benefits of forced protection against the rebellion that it inevitably engenders. Thus, forced protection is always a judgment call, and as with all judgment calls, the wisdom of the decision can be seen only in retrospect.

Whether or not forcing a teen into a treatment environment is wise often depends on the expertise of the staff at the treatment center. Whether or not forcing a teen to live with grandparents is a wise decision often depends on the grandparents' wisdom in handling the child and balancing that against their own needs.

In an analogous example, when a spouse forces a spouse into an alcoholic treatment center, the result is either beneficial due to treatment center expertise or backfires with increased spouse resentment if the treatment is unsuccessful. There are no "cut and dried" answers in such situations.

DEALING WITH REBELLION

The physical, cognitive, and psychological changes ripping through Tommy and Heather and all the other kids in the neighborhood converge to produce what is known as adolescent rebellion. As we've pointed out, rebellion is one way teens announce to themselves and others, "I am not my parent."

If teens have been given choices and a reasonable amount of control from years one through eleven, they have already established a healthy base of an identity independent of their parents. Kids raised this way often don't go through a rebellious phase at all.

The poor teens who have been raised in a drill sergeant environment—where Dad barked orders and kids obeyed—know only how to listen to an outside voice. They've never learned anything else. Children of helicopter parents aren't much better off, because their parents have protected them out of a warped understanding of love.

If the drill sergeant pattern has been predominant, Mom and Dad had better watch out when Joey gets into the eighth grade. As soon as Joey starts thinking abstractly, he switches from listening to his parents to listening to his peer group. Joey hasn't changed; he's still listening to a voice outside his head. But now somebody else is handing out instructions, and Joey's not thinking for himself.

But here's some good news for the drill sergeant and helicopter parents — which many of us tend to be because we were raised that way. Actually, there's good news and bad news. The good news is that if you got along well with your child from birth through age eleven, you have pretty good grounds for telling yourself, "It'll all work out all right . . . in the long run." Even if your child turns hard-core rebellious, if life was basically fine through age eleven you can take heart that things will turn out all right.

The bad news is that the long run may be a *very* long run. Some of these teens don't get through those rebellious years until they're around thirty.

Rebellion — Harmless or Destructive?

Consultant parents already know — and drill sergeant parents can learn — that a lot of adolescent "rebellion" is not self-destructive. Expressions such as haircuts or clothing styles are really quite safe, however weird or threatening they may seem to parents. In recent years, male teens have taken to having their ears pierced, and parents have once again been forced to learn how to cope with a new fashion.

Let's say college freshman Matt comes home and surprises his parents with an earring stuck in his left ear. His mom has a range of responses to choose from:

1. "YOU GET THAT THING OUT OF YOUR EAR RIGHT NOW BEFORE YOUR FATHER COMES HOME! WE DIDN'T RAISE OUR SON TO BE A HOMOSEXUAL!"
2. "Matt, why did you do this to us? Don't you love us?"
3. "Well, son, I'm sure it didn't cost as much as

when you got that pink Mohawk."
4. "What a lovely thing; maybe I ought to get one for myself."
5. "My male friends aren't into earrings, but I'm sure you know what's best for you."

Love-and-logic parents realize that although Matt may be trying to impress or shock his parents, more than likely he's just doing what his frat brothers are doing. These parents realize that most teens who do apparently "rebellious" things don't try to push them on others. Matt is not about to suggest, "Let's get Grandpa to pierce his ear."

When teens rebel in an isolated area but are generally responsible in other areas of their life, then it's okay for parents to acknowledge the behavior while not approving it. They can say to their teen, "This is my thought on it."

If rebellious activity is self-destructive, however, then it's *not* okay simply to accept the behavior. For example, if teens are abusing drugs or hanging out with a tacky friend who's been ripping off cars, then a parent should *neither approve nor accept* such activity. Parents can't control their teens in these activities, but they can say, "I don't want to see you with that friend around me. I don't want to see that cigarette dangling from your mouth."

Resist the Urge to Control

When your teen's rebellion gets in your face, resist the urge to control and switch to what *you're* going to do. If your teen wears an earring to get your goat, you can say calmly "not around me." In this way, you throw the consequence back on your teen while you take care of yourself.

If we come across as trying to control our children, it can injure our relationship. It's important that we recognize the potential resentment we may provoke with demands such as, "You're not going to do *that* around me!" Such comments put stress on the relationship, often with negative results. As we decide whether to overlook or actively oppose rebellious behavior, we must weigh the potential destructiveness of that behavior against the damage we might do to our relationship with our teen by opposing it.

LET THEM GO AND LET THEM GROW

We can help ourselves and our teens by understanding them from the inside out—recognizing and responding appropriately to the internal changes they all go through.

In general, despite the bewildering barrage of adolescent cognitive, physical, and psychological changes, and the rebellion that goes along with them, things are going to turn out okay. Children on the road to independence still want acceptance, even if they don't get approval. Teens generally don't ask for across-the-board approval, but they do need the deep assurance of being accepted for who they are—regardless of what they wear, what they do and who they do it with, or what they believe.

Parents who lean toward the drill sergeant mode in their need to control might be able to keep their teens from bolting out of the family's value system. But sadly, this can bear bitter fruit in later years as their childrens' marriages, families, and jobs disintegrate under pressure from a mid-life crisis because their children never learned to evaluate their values critically when they were younger.

If there's going to be a hard and critical look at values, better to have it occur now in adolescence than midway through life. Later, it will often mean a change of job, a change of spouse, and a rejection of the parenting role. As we're fond of saying, it's always cheapest to pay for a mistake today: tomorrow the cost goes up.

Parents, take a deep breath and trust that you have given your children what they needed in the first eleven years. Let go of your attempt to hold on to control (which you can't really keep anyway) and say to yourself, "My children are going to do things I don't approve of, but I accept them. I'm going to love my children on the faith that they know what they're doing. I may not like it, but I know that my children will have to live their own life."

(Teens themselves can help foster communication when they ask their parents what life was like for *them* as adolescents. This kind of exchange can have healthy results in greater understanding and respect between children and parents. And they just might learn something from each other, too!)

Keep in mind that your adolescent is going through a phase. But so are you—being a parent of an adolescent is also a transitional period. You're not the only one so worried about your teen, although it may feel that way sometimes. Relax and ride the changes through. Sure it may be a wild ride—but it can be a wonderful one, too.

7

UNDERSTANDING TEENS FROM THE OUTSIDE IN:
External Changes in Adolescence

❖

K ids grow up. They become parents. Their kids grow up and *they* become parents. On it goes.

So parenting should be simple, right? Just do what your folks did. Well, that would work great if we still lived in the same era our parents lived in.

When George was growing up, the most complex piece of electronics his family owned was a television. He saw his father snap pencils in half as he struggled to fill out IRS forms. And George was forever wishing his mother would put all her recipes in one place instead of frantically rummaging through the kitchen for a missing index card while she was halfway through cooking dinner.

George pursued a career and started a family of his own. His wife, Beth, had a full-time job. But the more they tried to get ahead, the more they seemed to slip behind.

So George bought a computer with programs for filing recipes, tracking automobile repairs, and completing tax forms. The more he found it could do, the more he did. Paradoxically, the computer made family life busier at the same time that it made family life easier.

The kids, fifteen-year-old Sharon and thirteen-year-old Bill, found that the family computer could make *their* lives easier, too. It sped up their homework. And it offered all kinds of games they could play—which started becoming an obsession each time they turned on the machine.

Times of study and recreation quickly degenerated into screaming matches between Sharon and Bill. During one heated argument, Bill knocked over a glass and spilled a soft drink into the hard drive. They lost not only the game, but everything stored on the hard drive as well.

George—who was staring at the April 15th tax deadline—lost it, too. "We didn't have computer games when I was your age!" he yelled at Sharon and Bill. "Now look what you've done!" George didn't understand that the same tool that made life easier could also make life more complicated.

That's how many of us approach technology. We appreciate what it can do for us, but we're not aware of its liabilities. We know it's changing our world, but we're not sure how and where it's taking us.

This uncertainty in facing the unknown pretty well describes the challenge of parenting in today's turbulent world. We can't just reach into the past and grab the tools we need for the present. In many ways, it's a brand new world out there.

Understanding our teens from the inside out gives us a foundation of knowing their special needs. But in order to identify how to wield appropriate parenting tools to *meet* those needs, we must understand our teens *from the outside in.*

THE PRESSURE OF SOCIAL CHANGE

The technological revolution isn't the only social force pressuring us to forge a new set of tools for parenting teenagers. We've also experienced a revolution in human rights. Our collective social conscience now acknowledges that it's wrong to discriminate against people on the basis of their age, race, religion, nationality, or gender. Groups have sprung up to champion children's rights, many of which are very important. There's no going back to the "good old days" — which often weren't really all that good anyway.

We've felt the pressure of social change — if not revolution — in other areas as well:

♦ *Relationships.* We no longer know our teens' friends the way we once did. Yet those friends have more influences on our children than our friends did on us a generation ago. Our teens need more ways to evaluate critically what others are telling them.

♦ *Media.* The "tube" was a fascinating curiosity for our parents' or grandparents' generation. Now it's a permanent fixture in daily life. Teens spend more time glued to the tube than they spend in the classroom, not to mention doing schoolwork. And video games — television's faithful sidekick — can quickly turn from a hobby into an obsession.

♦ *Trends.* Trends are even more trendy now than when we were scrambling to keep up. Many fads are harmless, such as clothing or hairstyles that give teens that chic "Planet X" look. Other trends, such as technological advances, occur with such dizzying frequency that they're disorienting. Still other trends, such as the sexual revolution, have had widespread and harmful effects.

◆ *Consumerism*. Peer pressure can terrify teens into demanding that their parents buy them $130 sneakers, or at least give them enough allowance so they can do it on their own. Advertising teases kids with the myth that personal satisfaction is just a purchase away.

◆ *Divorce*. One out of two marriages ends in divorce. Guess who gets caught in the middle?

◆ *Rising violence*. As our society becomes increasingly violent, that violence is reflected in and acted out in our homes. Children carry those scars for a lifetime and are dangerously prone to inflicting their pain on their children.

These and other changes have forced us into reevaluating what effective parenting is all about. We've been shocked into the awareness that we need new styles for teaching teens how to think and prepare for the future.

A couple of generations ago, a young person could expect to spend a lifetime in one career, if not in one job. Gender usually determined vocation: he dug the coal, smelted the ore, designed the bridges. She taught the classes, styled the (women's) hair, did the homemaking.

But the world is changing so fast that we can't prepare teens for life-long occupations. They will need to retrain themselves over and over as new developments force some occupations into obsolescence and bring new ones into existence. Instead we *can* prepare teens for the future by teaching them how to think, how to respond to the stressful influences they face, and how to make their own decisions and live with the consequences.

DIFFERENT CIRCUMSTANCES, SAME NEEDS

Although circumstances change, teens' needs stay remarkably constant from generation to generation. Before we take a closer look at the pressures from social forces, let's examine teens' fundamental needs in relation to the external changes they experience. Teens today, just like teens a generation or a century ago, have the same three basic needs for *control, affection,* and *inclusion.*

The Need to Feel in Control
All of us have a strong need to know we're in control of our lives. Without that assurance, we get anxious. So we will naturally do what it takes to restore the comfort of having a sense of power over our circumstances. Until we obtain that sense of control, we will remain in some kind of a battle to get it. Teens are no different from corporate vice presidents on this.

Recall that in chapter 4 we described the love-and-logic approach to parental control as, "Don't be greedy. Never take any more control than you absolutely need to have." The most effective parents surrender control thoughtfully by offering choices.

Car dealers have this down to a science. They know that a car dealership selling only cars soon will go out of business. Dealers who stay in business also sell *control* to their customers. They ask, "Do you want automatic or standard? Do you want a four-door or a hatchback? Do you want two- or four-wheel drive?" With every question, with every response, the dealer is sharing control with the buyer. This gives the buyer a feeling of power, so the buyer doesn't feel shut out of the deal. Car dealers know how to meet this need on their own terms.

Parents, however, often behave just the opposite of car dealers. They refuse to share control and power with their teens, especially in battles they can't win anyway. The more control they retain, the more frustrated they get. Their teens, who have no control, are even more frustrated—and that's when they get revenge.

For example, it's disastrous to have a power struggle over an issue like grades. Teens' basic need for control will kick in all too easily. They can't win when their parents are crabbing about that D and vaguely threatening them to shape up "or else." They feel powerless. Therefore, just to show that they *have* power, they'll get bad grades just to win the struggle.

Wise parents don't get mad and spark control battles. Instead, they shower teens with sadness over a bad grade. Teens will then seek control through other channels, rather than through fighting with parents. Instead of "I'll show them," it becomes, "What am I going to do about this grade?" This way, they must take control over their own studying.

The Need for Affection
We all need the assurance that other people care for us. When we don't get it, we may act in strange ways. Any office manager can tell you stories about what happens when a new guy comes in and gets more attention from management than the supervisor who's been there for five years. The old hand acts hostile and throws petty barbs. He complains about a lot of little things. Lines are drawn between old and new, and "office politics" take over.

Teens are no different from supervisors. In the classroom or on the team, teens who are assured of the teacher's or coach's care will take risks they would never endure for anyone else. On the other hand, teens who do not feel they're receiving affection will not do their work and will probably engage in antisocial behavior.

The Need to Feel Included
None of us wants to feel like an outsider. This is especially true of teens. They want to know they're an important part of the family, the committee, the peer group. When they feel they're not accepted they will respond, "I want to go where I'm appreciated, where I'm included, where I'm an important member, where I have some control in what goes on."

But there's a big paradox for teenagers in their quest for inclusion. On one hand, they want to be included as part of the family. On the other, they want to be independent, which means they do things that seem strange, if not hostile, to the family.

Simultaneous with their need for inclusion, teens will invariably do things to declare independence: getting a radical haircut; announcing, "I'm not having Thanksgiving here, I'm having it at my girlfriend's house"; hanging out at the mall with friends; or abusing sex or drugs.

The parents, in turn, react—which to the teen feels like rejection, whether it actually is rejection or not. At that moment, the teen feels loss of control, withdrawal of affection, and exclusion instead of inclusion.

To make matters worse, when the teen displays his unhappiness and bitterness because these needs are threatened, the *parents* feel that they're losing control, affection, and inclusion. Now we're into a very destructive cycle.

WHAT'S DIFFERENT TODAY

If these needs have remained constant through generations, then what's different about today?

One of the biggest shifts took place with the advent of the teen culture of the 1950s. Ever since, teenagers have had an expanding array of options for declaring independence. All those options, to a lesser or greater degree, appear scary to the adults who may react in a rejecting way.

I (Jim) attended a high school in the 1950s with three

thousand students. In those three years of high school, I saw only two kids drunk. Everyone who saw those two was repulsed and embarrassed. These days, many teens drink just to get drunk. Times have changed.

Teens express their independence today in ways that are very different from those their parents used. Each generation of parents must wrestle afresh with a whole new set of behaviors, values, and temptations teens throw at them in their pursuit of independence. No doubt these trends and fads will continue to have shock value. The trick is how parents deal with things they least expect.

PRESSURES FROM OUTSIDE THE HOME

We won't dwell on relatively harmless trends in pop culture, since they come and go so quickly. Instead, we'll explore the more significant external influences that can have profound impacts on how parents guide their children through adolescence. Following are a few that parents especially need to be aware of.

Changing Relationships

Parents often say, "My teen has changed so much. He used to listen to me, but he doesn't anymore. He only listens to his friends now."

That teen hasn't grown into a different person. He's still the same child he always was. But he's just gone through eleven or twelve years of listening to his parents. Now he's trying to figure out who he is. It seems to him that he's not going to solve that struggle unless he quits listening to the parental voice. The handiest substitute is the voice of his peers.

As we discussed in chapter 6, kids switch from concrete to abstract thinking at the time they enter adolescence. When that shift occurs, the budding teenager realizes, "I can think for myself."

How do we teach teens to think for themselves instead of listening to their peers? Starting as early in life as possible, by saying to them, "You have to decide." In other words, we train them to listen to a quiet voice inside their heads saying, "I have to decide that if I make a good decision, it's going to feel good; if I make a bad decision, it's going to feel rotten."

So when your teen comes in and says, "Well, my friend thinks this, this, and this," you can say, "Thanks for sharing. That's an interesting way to look at it. I wonder where she picked that up. What do you think?"

But too often we tend to react in the opposite way: "Gee, where does she get off thinking like that? That's crazy. What's the matter with her?" And that's scary to our own teens because they think, "Wow, if my parents criticize my friend, what'll they do to me?" Pretty soon they won't want to talk to you.

The Consumerism Crunch

"*Mom, can I have . . . ?*" How many times have you heard that—too many, right?

And of course, if you buy it for your teen, it's never quite good enough. Their friends always seem to have a better model, a flashier color, a more recent edition.

If you feel that you just can't win when you cave in to your teen's demands for more stuff, you're on to something: you *can't* win. The "best" is always about two feet—or $20, or $200—out of reach. Out of *your* reach.

Instead of indulging their teens' whims for more and better, love-and-logic parents do what they do in so many other areas of life: throw the issue back to the teen, the way real life always does.

Teenage consumers always seem to want *the best*. How can parents sidestep the consumerism crunch and let their teens handle the pressure instead? We suggest this rule: *No matter how affluent they may be, parents should never get their kids the best of anything.* Parents should let their teens know that they deserve the best, but they should always require their teens to pay the difference between "average" and "best," just as in real life.

When your teen tells you he wants an expensive item, say to him, "John, buy it." And John, of course, will answer, "But I can't afford it." And then you say, "Well, you're resourceful. If you want it I'm sure you can find a way to afford it."

Simultaneously with this kind of response, we should be teaching our children that the real values in life center on love for people, not the acquisition of things. That love must be extended to all, regardless of social or economic status. And that love must override pressures — from peers or advertising — to consume more things.

However, parents sometimes send decidedly mixed messages on this when they don't walk their talk. If they're driving a car that costs as much as a college education, they're wasting their time telling teens to resist peer pressure.

But even if your values are in place, it won't soften the vicious sting of peer pressure your children may feel when they aren't wearing the newest and hippest clothes. Regrettably, in some of our upscale communities all the teenagers have the very best. And for all the alleged refinement of those communities, teens can be mean and shove their affluence down the throats of their peers.

Some of that arrogant affluence gets downright ridiculous. The most outrageous example of conspicuous consumption we've come across lately is teens who leave price tags hanging out of their clothes so other kids can see how much they're worth.

We need to be careful in how we teach our teens proper values and a sober attitude toward possessions. We can set our kids up for problems if we buy them unfashionable clothes that make them look "weird" in the eyes of their peers. But that doesn't mean we have to go out and buy the best of the best. Let's use common sense.

Here's a sample conversation showing how a love-and-logic parent might handle a discussion about possessions.

"Mom," says Randy, "all the kids now are wearing Super Hi-Flight Pump-Up Get-Down Sneakers."

Mom low-keys it. "That's nice, dear."

"So when are you going to get me a pair? Can we go now? All the kids have them."

"*All* the kids, dear?"

"Well, not *all* — the dorks and nerds of course don't have them. But the parents of the *cool* kids get them the Super Hi-Flight Pump-Up Get-Down sneakers."

"And how much did they pay for those sneakers, Randy?"

"They cost a hundred and thirty dollars. For five bucks more you can get the day-glow laces, too."

Mom, of course, freezes inwardly in her financial tracks. But she keeps her cool. "Well, dear, you know that we want the best for you, but we can't afford them. We believe that you're smart and can work hard enough so if we give you the money for the sneakers we usually buy, you can earn the difference. Then you'll have the sneakers you want."

Randy, of course, is highly displeased with this answer. So he pushes the ultimate parent guilt button: "Mom, don't you love me?"

Mom doesn't fall for it. "Of course I do, dear. That's why we buy you average good sneakers and allow you to earn the money to get better ones if you wish."

Mom doesn't let on that she thinks the other parents are pushovers. Instead, she lets Randy know what her value system is without putting the other folks down.

"But Mom," Randy tries one last time, "what am I going to tell the other kids if I can't get the sneakers?"

Mom closes with an alternative: "Well, honey, you could tell them that you'd rather use the extra money for something else."

The more responsible our teens are, the more say-so we can allow them in what they wear. But if they're irresponsible, and they want to wear outlandish clothing or a green Mohawk, it's on their nickel.

Our teens may object to our approach and protest, "Well your value system stinks." We can reply, "Fine. That *is* my value system, and it's what allowed me to earn my money. So if you want to wear your green Mohawk, fine — go earn the money on *your* value system."

The Media Blitz

The media blitz is all around us — wide-angle, narrow-angle, pan right, pan left, up, down. Images flash before us: youth, sex, beauty, sex, conspicuous consumption, sex, music, sex, emotion, sex.

And if that isn't fast enough we can jump channels: click, click, click.

We live in a visual-media culture — don't blink, you'll miss the next image. The changes are happening not only *around* us, but also *to* us. Some are good, some are bad. But we need to be aware of them.

Before the current electronic and information revolutions, children had to read, and their minds would work faster than what was on that page. Their minds were compelled to visualize what they were reading. The same thing happened with radio. Broadcasters and radio actors told stories and read the news. Listeners used their imagination to form mental pictures.

Television dramatically changed that. The camera does the imaging — in astonishingly rapid succession. The mind doesn't have time to imagine, and it doesn't have to. The camera does all the work.

Teens in our television culture are conditioned to be passive while a machine does their mental work for them. If an activity involves thinking, perseverance, tedium, or patience, they call it "b-o-o-oring."

True, the proliferation of technological and media wizardry has brought tremendous benefit. We can see our world, literally, as never before. We can understand more of what's happening in it. And we can communicate with space-age speed and accuracy.

But these benefits have come embedded in a barrage of information and images. The blitz is not slowing down. And it's bringing with it plenty that is *not* of benefit. Battles are raging over what kids are exposed to in network and cable TV programming.

In a highly technical world, relationships are often the first things to drop out. We can't stop the barrage. But we can maintain the sanity and solidity of relationships in the family. We can make it a point to create family time in which we can talk to each other without the background buzz of the tube. We can do more reading, setting an example for our teens. We can express excitement about what we're learning and how we're learning it. We can ask our teens what they see in their videos and movies, and we can discuss the lyrics and music of the songs they listen to. Reading and discussion also meets the basic needs of control, affection, and inclusion.

RIDING THE WAVES OF TRENDS

Remember the Lambada, the hot dance craze of '88 to '89? It was sexy, it was fast, it was daring. It is history.

Pop culture can be very alluring. Trends and fads tend to spice things up. Kids are especially attracted to them because they temporarily fill needs for control, affection, and inclusion. They offer a quick fix for expressing independence and winning approval and acceptance from peers.

Most of what teens do to demonstrate their independence will soon be replaced by something else. The streaking fad popular on college campuses in the early seventies died out because people quit looking at it. If you're independent, and no one is noticing, what's the point?

If nobody seems to notice your purple hair, you find another way to show your independence. This quest for independence has gone on in all cultures at all times. Parents shouldn't worry about fads and trends that really are harmless.

Some trends, however, have much more serious and long-term effects, such as eighth-graders packing pistols, or the rising incidence of early sexual activity. The fifties, sixties, and seventies ushered in a wave of increasing sexual activity among children in their upper teens. In the eighties and nineties, this wave is reaching down to children in their lower teens and below. There's a trickle-down effect as teens engage in more adult behavior at increasingly younger ages.

As our culture absorbs things that are faddish or even shocking, we tend to relax our tolerance. When I (Jim) first saw the movie *Psycho*, the shower scene shocked me so much that I couldn't sleep for a month. When I saw it again years later, I partially closed my eyes to avoid looking at it but wasn't phased by what I saw. I've been so desensitized by what's happened in our culture that the horrible image of a woman getting stabbed to death in a shower didn't bother me much.

The magic of love-and-logic parenting is that teens raised in this parenting style express their independence through responsible decision-making. This expression satisfies their need for control, earns teens respect and affection, and includes them as equal members of the family.

Love-and-logic teens are normal kids. Sure, they'll probably pick up on trends as quickly as the next kid. But they're not driven to socially deviant behavior in order to demonstrate that they're individuals. (When teens do adopt such deviant behaviors, however, we should let the full weight of the law come down on them, just as the law would come down on us.)

PRESSURES FROM INSIDE THE HOME

Life After Divorce

The effects of divorce on teens have been widely chronicled, and we don't pretend to offer a deep analysis here. We will, however, offer some love-and-logic tips for divorced parents.

Single parents have an especially tough time of raising children. These children have particular needs for love and acceptance, especially when they reach their teenage years. However, they also know that because they have one less parent to deal with, they have the opportunity to seize control of the family situation—and cause a lot of damage in the process.

We offer the following thoughts for single parents to keep in mind as they raise teenagers:

First make time for yourself, then make time for your kids. If you burn yourself out, you'll have nothing left to give to your children. Schedule time for yourself alone as well as with your children. If it helps, think of these times as dates. Then make them a priority.

Just because your children are growing up in a single-parent home doesn't mean they're doomed to troubled relationships later in life. Single moms, your attitudes toward men will heavily influence what kind of man your son will be, or how your daughter will regard men.

Separate what you can control from what you can't and then learn to live with both. You can work on what you *can* control. For what you *can't,* tell yourself, "I don't like it but I can't control it."

For example, all parents—including single parents—are in control of their gifts of love, their smile, their touch, and their joy at their teens' achievements. And parents are in control of their own reactions when their children are disrespectful or experience life's difficulties. Controlling things that go on outside the parental skin, however, is much more difficult. In the long run it is best to adjust your attitudes to put up with it rather than trying to change something that's out of your control.

Single parents who remarry have another parent in the family. Serious problems can occur when parents want to do the right thing but don't know how to resolve the tensions between their new spouse and the children. In a stepparenting situation, everyone feels caught in the middle. This tension experienced by stepchildren is so deeply ingrained that fairy tales are filled with it.

In such families, parent and stepparent must make very clear to the children that the couple's relationship is primary. The birth parent holds the key to maintaining harmony. He or she has to let the teens know that the most important thing is the person he or she is spending the rest of his or her life with. If a discipline problem arises, the birth parent must unequivocally back up the stepparent as an authority in the home.

When a parent remarries and the family becomes "blended," the most common problem in the reconstituted family is *triangulation*. This means that everybody feels caught in the middle. If the mother is the birth parent, she feels caught between her own children and her new spouse. Her husband feels caught between the wife he loves and her obnoxious children. And, of course, the children feel caught between their mom and the stepdad. They may initially feel less loved and, more significantly, less respected.

The key to the triangulated situation lies with the response of the birth parent. The birth parent must make it absolutely clear to the children that her allegiance and love lies with her new husband—the person she will be spending the rest of her life with. Unfortunately, it is sometimes true that the children, consciously or unconsciously, wish things were "back the way they were before Mom remarried" and may want to have their birth parent all to themselves. At this point, it is a wise birth parent who lets the children

know, unequivocally, that, should family problems escalate, if anyone were to go, it would *not* be the new spouse!

A good relationship between child and stepparent is
healthy and worth striving for. But when disputes arise,
the birth parent must not take the child's side in arguments
with the stepparent and validate the child's anger. The birth
parent must make an important judgment before remarry-
ing: "If I think the person I'm going to marry isn't going
to be a good authority figure for my children, I shouldn't
marry that person."

Breaking the Cycle of Violence
Our society is becoming more violent partly because more
children are experiencing more violence earlier in their
lives. Often, we can't directly control or change many of
the causes of youth violence, such as easy access to weapons.
But we can influence how we parent our children.

Poor early parenting often starts a cycle of neglect,
rebellion, and irresponsibility in children who grow older
without growing up. These children haven't learned to live
with the consequences of their wrong decisions. When they
in turn have children themselves, poor early parenting is
repeated in succeeding generations until someone breaks
the cycle.

When people have not had the opportunity to learn
how to make decisions and live with the consequences, they
don't know how to cope responsibly with seemingly difficult problems, especially related to child-raising. Instead of
thinking clearly, they lash out in anger. Instead of reasoning
with their teens, they will revert to a harsh drill sergeant
style of parenting. When their children make mistakes, they
turn to physical abuse.

Teens who grow up in such families learn no other
way to deal with their frustration—or, in the future, with
their children's frustrations. Yet all along, these children,
and especially teenagers, caught in this cycle often know

in their hearts that these family dynamics are wrong.

Many parents find themselves getting angrier and more frustrated than they know they should be. For those who recognize inappropriate anger and desire to change, here are three suggestions for dealing with it:

1. *Be open about your problem with other family members and with those in your community who can help.* Covering up domestic violence only increases the shame parents feel, exacerbating the cycle. Many churches, community centers, and social service agencies have support groups to help parents who are caught in this cycle of violence. Parents and teenagers caught in the web of domestic violence should not hesitate to seek help from professional counselors.

2. *Get ideas, tools, and techniques from other individuals and support groups who can help you with your problem.* For example, one such technique is: If you're so mad that you don't know what to say, don't say anything until you've cooled off.

If you lose control and yell at your teen, by definition you have just given control to your teen—because you've lost it. That's not good for either of you. If you're angry but you stop to think it over and then decide to say something, keep your voice down. This is good for you and your teen.

Once you can control your own emotions, you're in a good position to help others control theirs.

3. *Commit yourself to working toward the necessary internal change that will give you the discipline to apply techniques for controlling your anger.* This inner desire is the true starting point for breaking the cycle of violence. Techniques are helpful when they're built on the inner determination and discipline to resist violent behavior.

This internal change takes place with prayerful meditation on the recognition that you do have the resources to change. Focus on the anticipation of improving, not on the defeat of repeating the pattern. Instead of saying, "Oh, Lord, grant me more patience with Jennifer," which zeros in on what you *don't* have, say, "Lord, thanks for those three seconds I had patience with Jennifer," which builds on what you *do* have. Over time, that three seconds can grow to three minutes, and then to three hours.

SAVE YOUR EMOTIONAL ENERGY

We've outlined only a few of the external influences on family life that affect teenagers. No book can cover them all. And even if it did, it would be immediately obsolete because of the rapid developments in technology, trends, and social ills. We don't have much control over what goes on outside our influence. But we can control and love our own corner of the world. That means we have some decisions to make about the energy we have.

Each of us has only so much emotional energy. Imagine an emotional "energy pie," the whole pie representing 100 percent of our emotional energy. If I spend 80 percent of my emotional energy focusing on what's wrong with the world and complaining that nobody's doing anything about it, I have only 20 percent of my energy left for my teenagers.

However, if I spend 10 percent of my energy observing how the world is changing and another 10 percent in legitimate efforts to change it, I can direct up to 80 percent to help mold the future of my teens.

Each of us needs to make a conscious decision about how we will divide up all our emotional pie. Love-and-logic parents spend the majority of their energy on the family.

You and your children will outlast any hairstyles and dance crazes. You will witness profound changes in technology and politics. Devote yourself to what is of greatest and lasting importance: strengthening your most intimate contacts with spouse, parents, and children. You and your family will not only survive the pressure of external forces, but you may even have opportunity to shape those forces as well.

8

READY, SET —
Off into the Real World

❖─────────

S ooner than you think, your teenager will walk out of your life and into the real world. It's pretty normal to feel that you're losing control as your teen gets older. That's the idea. You're not supposed to have that kind of control.

Parenting is all about raising a child who is thoughtful, capable, and loving, able to go out in the world and make it. Whatever you can give your teens to help them reach that point is what counts. The thank-you's and "what a great parent you were" and "oh, how I'll always love you!" are, quite frankly, frosting on the cake of life.

As a love-and-logic parent, you're cultivating relationships with your children in which there's room to negotiate. You're developing a friendship with your teen in which you can speak to your youngster as a young adult: "How can we help each other through these tough times? How do we get you ready to live in that real world out there so that you've had enough practice and there are no big surprises when you get there?"

But just as you say that, another practice opportunity comes along. Your son Larry wants to borrow a hundred bucks from you.

You know that the real world doesn't hand out C-notes. So you say, "Sure, I'll loan you a hundred dollars. No problem. What do you have for collateral?"

"Collateral?" Larry puzzles. "What's that?"

"Well, Larry, that's something of yours I hold on to so that if you don't pay me back by the end of the month, it's no big deal because I can sell your property."

"Why, I don't—I don't have anything like that."

"Sure you do," you reply matter-of-factly. "You have your stereo or your skis."

"You mean you'd sell *those*?" Larry asks fearfully.

"Well, not if you paid back the loan by the time we agreed upon. That's the way the bank deals with me. Otherwise, sure I'd sell the stereo. Or I could donate it to charity and get a tax write-off. It's no big deal. And then you won't owe me a thing, see? And we'll both be happy."

Larry balks—"Uh, maybe I don't really need the loan after all."

WELCOME TO THE REAL WORLD

"Welcome to the real world," you were telling Larry. That was a loving thing to do. Easy money with no strings attached is *not* what the real world offers to us. Love is a beautiful and lovely thing, but it can mess things up when it's wrongly applied as unrealistic protection.

To introduce our kids to the real world, we have to observe what happens there. In the real world where we all live, why do we get our chores done? Why do we do our work? Yes! Because we get paid. Why do we like getting paid? Because we like eating and having a roof over our heads.

Larry will find this out firsthand when he gets his own apartment or moves in with friends in college or after graduation. What are the rules there? Only the rules that he makes, right?

If you want Larry to be independent, does that mean you give him total run of the house? Can he go anywhere he wants to without your knowing where he is, when he's coming home? Can he freely disregard the rest of the family's rights? Of course not.

Larry, like most teens his age, has young, healthy eardrums. He likes his music loud. He likes to blast his stereo through the house so that the walls shake. It's more exciting than just wearing the earphones.

So you say, "Hey Larry, I don't like the music this loud in the house."

Larry retorts, "Well, you know, it's my house, too!"

You reply with real-world wisdom, "Check the mortgage, Larry, and look at who signed it. This is *my* house. When you grow up, you'll have your own house. Then you can listen to the music *you* want — your name will be on that mortgage, not mine. But right now, this is my house."

From this exchange, Larry learns that he has responsibilities toward other family members as long as he lives at home, and will have rights of his own when he buys his own house.

TECHNIQUES FOR WORLD-WISE TEENS

It's never too late to start changing your parenting techniques, even if you've been a helicopter parent hovering over your teen with overprotective love or a drill sergeant parent mandating top-down authoritarianism. The following practical suggestions are things you can work on together with your teen to prepare him or her for the final years in your house—and for the real world.

Three Rules for Teenagers
We suggest that you set out these three rules for your teenager to follow:

> *Rule 1.* Treat me with the same respect you gave me when you were in elementary school. In other words, I expect respect.

> *Rule 2.* I expect you to do your chores around the house.

> *Rule 3.* If you have average intelligence, you need to get overall average grades in school. That means that if you don't do well in chemistry and algebra, you can pull up your average to achieve the appropriate grade point by doing well in other courses that are not so difficult.

Three Messages for Teenagers
Those three rules are backed by three messages you should give your teens:

> *Message 1.* I love you.

> *Message 2.* If you have any questions, ask.

> *Message 3.* Good luck in life.

That "good luck" message has tremendous power to it. It actually empowers your teens by letting them know that they have the responsibility to solve their own problems. It says, "Well, that's your problem. It's not my problem." The sweet way to say "That's your problem" is to wish the teen good luck.

Let's say Jessica has been slacking off in her seventh-grade studies, and her teachers have been talking about holding her back for a year.

You comment, "Jessica, the way you study, I've been thinking about how you're going to get pretty familiar with the seventh grade. And honey, I just want to take this opportunity to wish you luck."

"Oh [moan]." Jessica feels how scary it is for her mom to just come up and wish her luck, because now she realizes that she has to do something about it.

If parents worry and agitate about something, by definition their child doesn't have to.

Four Steps to Responsibility

One of the ironies of parenting is that the best way to influence teens to become irresponsible and fail at life is to become highly involved in making sure that they *do* make it. This is because the implied message in that involvement is, "I don't think you're going to succeed, so I'd better get in here." And the teen lives up to that.

Overly involved parents who intrude on their children's lives from kindergarten through twelfth grade will almost always raise learning-resistant children.

To help your teen, and give yourself a break in the process, follow these four steps to responsible offspring:

Step 1. Give your teen a responsibility.

Step 2. Trust that your teen will carry it out, and at the same time hope and pray that she blows it. Because that's how she'll learn the most from it. If she blows it today, there's a learning experience at the end of it.

Of course, hoping she'll blow it doesn't mean you'll be sending messages that she's worthless and can't think for herself. It's just that the cost of her mistake is cheaper today than she will ever have to pay to learn that lesson in the real world.

Step 3. When she does blow it, stand back and allow consequences to occur while expressing empathy.

Step 4. This is the most important one: Turn right around and give her that same responsibility all over again, because that sends the powerful implied message, "You're so smart that you can learn. People do learn from their mistakes, and you're no different. I'm sure you'll learn from yours, too."

That beats the parent who criticizes by communicating, "You blew it! Now I have to do it." The powerful implied message here is, "You're so dumb you can't learn from what happened."

Encourage Your Teen
Building responsibility isn't a cold-hearted system. We need to encourage our teens by helping them draw strength from what they do well. This can help them rise to the challenge of handling difficult areas.

One mom asked our advice in dealing with her daughter, who wasn't much of a student academically but was very involved in sports.

We told her to take the thing that her daughter could do the best and encourage her to do that with everything she had. We felt that would charge up her daughter's batteries so that she could feel strong enough to try some other things she felt weak in.

So her mom asked, "How can I help best? Can I help you best by nagging you, reminding you, staying out of it, helping you with your strengths?"

"Well, Mom," the daughter replied, "I like running track and I'm really good at it. It means a lot to me when you come to the meets and watch me. I'm really struggling now with English. I appreciate whatever help you can give me, but please don't nag."

Her daughter told her what kind of help she needed. But focusing on her strengths is what gave her the boost.

Never take away from teens what they *can* do well until they improve in activities they don't do well. Otherwise they will suffer the discouragement of not being able to point to *anything* they can do well.

Getting to "No"

We have the right to expect our children to live the way we want them to live, and sometimes that means saying "no." The three basic rules for saying "no" — which cuts down on adolescent rebellion later — are:

1. *Say no as seldom as possible.* Don't use the word if you don't need to.
2. *Say no as much as necessary.* Use the word if you must.
3. *Mean business when you say no.*

A lot of teens have trouble with "no." But if we use it sparingly, it will mean more when we do say it.

As teens grow older, we may have to say "no" with one form or another of tough love. For example, "These are my simple requirements: doing your chores, earning decent grades, and treating me with respect. They're pretty simple. If you can't meet them then I'm sad for you, and you may need to look for a place to live where you like the rules."

We have a responsibility as parents and an obligation to our children to expect and require responsible behavior. That's not the same as demanding blind obedience. Also, if we keep teens focused on how they can meet expectations for responsible behavior, they're less likely to be dwelling on how they can get their way.

Whose Problem Is It?

Child psychiatrists stay busy answering the question: *Who owns a problem? Is it the teen's problem or is it the parents' problem?* I (Foster) will tell you directly, that if every parent were able to separate out whether it was the child's problem or their own problem, the average child psychiatrist would soon be out of business.

Parents' problems are those that directly affect them:

◆ Chores not being done.
◆ Loud music.
◆ Teens coming home late or not being home when they're supposed to be there.
◆ Being awakened by teens in the middle of the night.

Teens' problems do not directly affect parents:

◆ Losing schoolbooks and clothes. Protective parents goof here because they say, "Well, I'm the one who pays for those things." They don't go the next step and say, "I'm the one who paid for the *first* one of those."
◆ Bad grades in school.
◆ Choice of friends—unless there's a party at home with inappropriate activity.
◆ Bedtime schedules.

This is not a theoretical exercise. If we *don't* separate out who owns these problems, we'll have rebellious teenagers. And we'll also get mad at them for something they've done to themselves.

Any time somebody gets mad at you for something you've done to yourself, it makes the problem worse. Let's say you're putting up a picture, using a hammer, and by accident you haul off and whack your thumb. Someone else comes along and remarks, "You dummy — you shouldn't have done that! Didn't I warn you about that? That's such a careless thing to do. . . ." This does not help. It only makes the problem worse. You will probably start thinking about what else you would like to hit with the hammer.

Joe recently shelled out several months' pay for his daughter Shelly's braces. He notices that Shelly has not been brushing her teeth.

"Shelly, I've become aware that you're not brushing your teeth," says Joe. He does *not* say, "I paid a lot of money for those braces. You better brush your teeth! Look at what you're doing to your gums." Joe knows that would only make the problem worse.

So Joe continues, "The nice thing about braces, Shelly, is they can be put on when you're an adult or when you're thirteen. Right now, as a matter of fact, there are a zillion orthodontists making money on adults, putting the tin in their grin. The advantage of having braces when you're thirteen is that I pay for them. The disadvantage, for you, of having braces when you're an adult is that *you* pay for them."

Joe then turns empathetic, with a dose of humor: "But it will be sad when you go to high school and college, and you want to kiss someone but he says, I don't want to kiss you; you're Fang Face! And every time you'd kiss him, you'd poke him with your incisors. That would be hard on him."

Finally, Joe drives home the consequences of Shelly's failure to brush, but leaves the decision up to her by saying, "If the brushing doesn't improve, the next visit to the dentist, your braces come out."

Shelly pleads, "Please — I want my braces! I don't want to be Fang Face!"

Joe concludes without anger and with great kindness, "Well, we'll see. But if there's no brushing, the braces come out."

PARENTING PERSPECTIVES
ON REAL-WORLD READINESS

As you work to apply the above techniques, keep in mind the following perspectives on helping your teens get ready for the real world.

**One Month of Love-and-Logic Covers
a Year's Multitude of Sins**
Some readers may have been applying love-and-logic principles for years, while others—such as drill sergeant or helicopter parents—are being introduced to them for the first time. If these principles are new to you, you may wonder if you will ever be able to apply them before your teen flies the nest.

We've found that when parents start applying love-and-logic principles, it takes about one month of choices and consequences to correct one year of drill sergeant or helicopter parenting. We base this calculation of the one-month-to-one-year correction rate on a simple observation of college students.

On average, teenagers are eighteen when they go off to college. We've observed a typical pattern among those who have been protected by helicopters or bossed by drill sergeants during those eighteen years. They tend to flounder through their freshman year, the following summer, and the first semester of their sophomore year. By the time they reach the second semester of year two, they finally start pulling it together.

That's eighteen months to correct eighteen years of poor patterns of personal responsibility. By applying love-and-logic principles as soon as possible, those eighteen months in college will lessen. Think of it as an investment in your teenager's college tuition. The sooner your teen begins to act responsibly, the more he or she will participate in and benefit from a college education.

United You Stand, Divided You Fall

It's important for parents to present a united front. In essence, here's the rule of thumb: The more irresponsible the teen, the more important it is for the parents to agree on the discipline they use. The healthier the teen, the more the parents can agree to disagree openly in front of the teen by saying, "Well, we have different ideas. This is how your mom feels, and I back her to the hilt." If you have a disturbed child or a difficult child, then the united front must be absolute, with no cracks in it: "This is where we stand. Period."

Most parents find ways to work through their disagreements over discipline. Sometimes, however, they may reach an impasse. Or they may throw up their hands and say, "We just can't handle this problem." This is a good time to seek help from individuals or organizations who can help identify the issues and suggest approaches that have worked for other parents in similar situations.

If the parents themselves have disturbed personalities and try to enforce inappropriate rules, however, a tough love approach will fail because they will not have earned the respect of their teens.

Save Punishment

What we're about to say sounds a little strange, because we believe in law and order. But here it is anyway: *There's no room in this love-and-logic philosophy for punishment – none at all.*

Of course, this immediately prompts all sorts of protests. "Hey, wait a minute. You expect teens to behave. You expect them to be responsible. Yet you don't believe in punishment?" True, we don't. Then parents say, "You mean you *never* use punishment?" Well, we're human, too. We haven't arrived at the point where we can always settle a problem or help a teen without using punishment. The only problem is every time we use punishment, we don't feel very good about ourselves. Stay with us as we try to explain.

There are two ways of hurting: from the outside in, and from the inside out. Hurting from the outside in only goes skin deep. It occurs when someone else is angry or when teens can't make a connection between the infraction and the parent's response. It just doesn't sink in. This occurs when the response is not something that would happen to an adult in the real world.

Instead of punishment, we use "the concept of hurting from the inside out." We allow children to suffer the consequences of their decisions so that every time they ask themselves this question — "Who's making me hurt like that?" — they have to turn around and say, "Oh, me."

For example, Paul's parents get angry about his report card and ground him, but it doesn't sink in because he makes no logical connection. John's parents say, "Wow, no more good student discount for your car insurance. You'll probably want to pay the difference so you can still drive."

Paul knows that grounding is punishment. Yet how many adults in the last two years have been grounded? It doesn't happen in the adult world. And it doesn't work with teens. Paul simply hurts from the outside in. No lessons, no change, no growth.

The same principle goes for washing out your teenagers' mouths with soap when they swear. Neither your boss nor your spouse will wash out your mouth with soap when you swear. But they may avoid you or tell you politely to clean up your language, which will make you hurt from the inside out. There's a good chance you'll learn a lesson here.

Whenever we lay something on teenagers that doesn't happen in the real world, it's almost bound to be a punishment and not a consequence. But we all operate by consequences. If we do a lousy job, we get fired. If we don't make our car payments, the bank repossesses the car.

We (Foster and Jim) oppose punishment because it doesn't lead to self-examination. Instead, it leads to resentment. When teens hurt from the inside out by correctly suffering the consequences of their actions, they examine their actions. This takes some thought, because laying down consequences is not always a natural thing for us. We may have to stop and reflect on what would happen in the real world in order for us to identify what the consequences should be for our teen.

As an alternative to punishment, give a lot of thought to how you can reinforce positive behavior, look for solutions, help your child reach his or her own conclusions, and allow the natural consequences to occur.

Angry? Bite Your Tongue

Many of us want to know, "How do I learn to come across without the booming voice, the anger, and the threats?" Some of us tell ourselves, "I'm not going to yell anymore." And then we find ourselves right back there again, that awful voice coming out of our mouths that we hate to hear. Our children hate to hear it, too.

The nice thing about teenagers is that if we don't properly apply a love-and-logic principle today, they're certain to give us another opportunity tomorrow. Sometimes it helps to say to yourself over and over just before you fall asleep at night, *When I get angry, I'm going to whisper. When I get angry, I'm going to whisper.* You can mentally rehearse as well. You may find that lo and behold, when your teen gives you another opportunity to react, you're able to handle it much more calmly.

Here are three principles that may help you bite your tongue instead of lash out with it when you're angry:

Principle 1. If it's not an emergency, it doesn't have to be handled right then. So we can say to our teens, "Unlucky for you, I'm angry. Lucky for you, I'm not going to talk to you about it until tomorrow." We let them know we're going to talk with them the next day.

Principle 2. Generally speaking, the angrier you are, the more important it is to lower your voice.

Principle 3. Talk it over with other people before you decide what to do. The consequence is usually better if it comes after both you and the teen have entered the "thinking state" after leaving the "emotional state."

I (Foster) think parents these days don't use each other as much as those in earlier decades who were surrounded by extended family or a close-knit community. Instead of going to a professional, many parents can look up someone in the neighborhood who has really great teens and ask them for advice. A mom could say to another mom, "You know, yesterday Susan said she would be in at midnight. She didn't come in until one-thirty a.m. She gave a lame reason, and I haven't done anything or said anything about it. You seem to have really neat kids. If your kids did that, what would you do?" Most of us would feel pleased and privileged if someone in our community asked us what we would do with our teens because they like the way our teens behave. This kind of networking is a good way to get advice and make new friends in the process.

The most appropriate time to reason with teenagers is when they're not in an emotional state. Even though they may act flippant and say, "I don't care," they still harbor plenty of emotion in controversial situations. If we try to communicate in the midst of a heated exchange, however, chances are they'll never hear the words we say. And we'll probably end up wishing we could take those words back anyway.

I (Foster) made it a point to deal with my teens in contexts when we were both happy. Usually, the best time for us was when we were driving out on the highway (and our child couldn't step out of the car and get away). We were reasonably happy, and I could introduce the subject by saying, "Oh, yeah, remember the other night? What were your thoughts about that? Let me tell you my thoughts." And we usually had a pretty decent conversation at that point. If we had tried that when we were both mad, nothing or worse than nothing would have happened.

Another caution about anger is to avoid handing down a consequence to your teen while you're angry, because it may be too strong and you'll want to change your mind once you've cooled down later on. If this happens very often, your teen may lose respect for you. Once that respect is lost, everything is a downhill slide from there.

If we've come down on our teens too hard, we can say, "I'm sorry I did that. I've given it more thought, and I'm thinking maybe I made a mistake. Here's what I think might be better. . . ." But that can only be done a few times, or we will form a pattern of inconsistency.

When parents are inconsistent, teens usually respond in one of three ways: (1) they get the impression that their parents shoot from the hip without thinking things through; (2) they wonder if their parents are basically pushovers; (3) they doubt whether their parents have their best interests at heart.

If you're concerned about being inconsistent with your teen, you might try this approach: "I'm wondering if I've come across inconsistently with you — telling you something one day and changing my mind the next. I don't think that helps you very much, so I'm going to try to do less of that. If you notice that I'm being inconsistent, you may want to remind me about it an a thoughtful way." But keep in mind that your teen may bring it up only when it's in his or her favor to do so.

Air Out Your Disagreements

As parents, most of us have learned by now that we're not always right. If we have a responsible teenager, and he's bent out of shape about something we've done or said, he probably has a legitimate grievance.

When I (Foster) have seen teens really hacked off at parents, they're usually right. I ask them, "Are you seeing red? Why are you feeling this way?"

When something's going on in the family that family members are trying to keep secret—telling the teen that this shouldn't be talked about with *anyone*—it's a red flag that it should be talked about with *someone*. That's the issue that's crippling the family, so that's the issue that should be dealt with.

When we tell our teens not to talk about something, we're ensuring that they're not going to be able to work it through. Because then they lose no matter what: If they don't talk, they don't resolve it; if they do talk, they suffer guilt over violating a parental injunction. A mandate of secrecy subconsciously cripples our teens.

When parents and teens have a disagreement, it's best to air them out by getting an outside opinion both parties respect. The best person is someone who's raised great teens, a youth counselor, or a professional counselor.

Keep Some of Your Curiosity to Yourself

Parents naturally want to know everything about what's going on with their teen. Interest can become inordinate curiosity, however, and questions can quickly turn into interrogations.

If you feel uncomfortable that you're questioning an

awful lot, perhaps you should keep some of your curiosity under wraps. Ask yourself, "Is it really any of my business? Would I be better off not knowing everything about my teen?"

There are a lot of things we'd like to find out from our teens that would devastate us if we learned the answer to them. Why not just let teens have a certain amount of their lives that's private? We can probably live happily for the rest of our lives in ignorance of some of those things.

There are probably several reasons why your teens don't share everything with you. First, they figure you might not be able to handle what they tell you. Second, they may feel that what they say would be too different from the way you see things. Third, they probably don't have a real good handle on how they feel or how to express themselves. All in all, they most likely feel a little inadequate sharing some things with you.

Our rule of thumb is to give incomplete sentences (which is a form of questioning) or we ask questions when we truly want that teen to think, not when *we* want the information. There's a big difference between the two. It's pretty obvious to teens whether we're truly trying to help them think something through, or just prying to satisfy our curiosity.

Questioning can be more comfortable if you start with an open-ended question, you thank them for sharing their response, and clarify whether you understand their responses correctly — for example, "Is this the way you're really feeling?" Other suggestions for opening conversations include:

- "It seems to me that. . . ."
- "I've noticed. . . . Do you have any thoughts on that?"
- "I'm pleased that you did well on. . . . What did you think about it?"

Often, parents are afraid to comment on what they're seeing or hearing because they're afraid they will chase their teens away. If your teens are hesitant to talk, don't force it. Show that you trust them, and allow them to talk on their own. Your conversations will be much more meaningful.

Say No Thanks to Guilt
Too often parents feel like failures if their teens don't measure up. They shouldn't. When teens have trouble, it doesn't necessarily mean the fault belongs to the parent.

Matters aren't helped if communities that should provide support cut parents down in their efforts. We know of a church that denied a man the opportunity to become a deacon because his daughter became pregnant out of wedlock. He hadn't been a lousy father. The daughter got pregnant, not the father. That church wasn't being fair about where the lines of responsibility are. It should have been supportive of the man.

Getting ready for and living in the real world means that we learn to take responsibility for our own actions. If you've done all you can for your child, and the child still makes harmful decisions, you should rest in the knowledge that you did your job. You're not a failure. Your child chose those decisions. When guilt comes calling through this door, say "thanks, but no thanks."

READY, SET, GO!

Our children are the most precious and valuable gifts our Creator can give us. We have eighteen short years to prepare them for real life. Once they're teens, the window of time is even smaller—but it's a window nonetheless.

Let's spend more time thinking about how we're going to parent our teenagers and what we can learn from them, and less time thinking about what might go wrong.

Ready, set, off into the real world! Parenting achieves its

major goal when teens leave home and go out into the world able to cope with it and make productive contributions. If your teen can exercise his or her own judgment, make decisions, and live with the consequences, rest assured that you've done your part.

Over time, your children will love and respect you more and more for teaching them how to think and how to live. As their maturity catches up to yours, you will discover that you can meet on common ground as adults, and that you have become friends. This is the greatest reward any parent can hope for.

Best wishes on your journey through life together.

PART III

Love-and-Logic
Parenting Pearls

Pearl 1

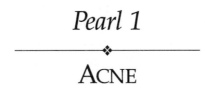

ACNE

Oh, no – zits!

Most teenagers will experience acne, and it's no laughing matter. Any flaw in the way teens look becomes magnified in their eyes. To most people, that blemish on a teen's face looks about three millimeters across. To the teen, it looks about three yards across.

We need to take our teens' feelings about their appearance seriously. It doesn't help when we casually toss off "Oh, honey, no one notices that," or "Don't worry—you'll grow out of it!" A teen reacts to a zit the way a successful adult responds to personal bankruptcy.

The jury is still out on what precisely causes acne. Doctors and scientists think that it comes from a combination of a genetic predisposition to acne, poor skin hygiene, allergies, a possible lack of sunlight, and fluctuations in hormones during adolescence.

We do know that massive hormonal changes during adolescence affect the production of a fatty lubricant in the skin called sebum. When skin pores and hair follicles clog with sebum and become infected by bacteria, acne results. Often it shows up in just a few isolated pimples, but in extreme cases it can lead to lesions and permanent scarring.

There's no sure way to tell which teens will be affected, but studies have shown that boys are more likely to suffer from acne than girls.

Teens' dramatic reactions to acne are in part due to the hormones that produce it. Their hormonal fluctuations are analogous to what new mothers experience in postpartum depression. Teens have not yet reached adult hormone balance, and their emotions follow the ups and downs of their seismic physiological changes.

So what can be done to help quiet the groans when they look in the mirror?

Teens will discover that their changing skin condition requires an accompanying change in cleansing habits. What was good enough for a nine-year-old doesn't cut it for a thirteen-year-old. Nine-year-olds can go several days without a shower; thirteen-year-olds can't. The same goes for washing their faces.

If normal hygiene doesn't clear up acne, parents and teens should seek medical care. Medication is now available that wasn't on the market a generation ago. There are plenty of over-the-counter commercial astringents and medications for controlling acne. In some cases, a physician may need to examine and treat the skin. Doctors can prescribe antibiotics such as tetracycline to deal with more severe cases, although frequent use may make bacteria resistant to such medication. Other drugs such as tretinoin or isotretinoin may be applied, but they may cause side effects.

Parents can reassure their teens that they are loved while telling them, "Who you are is more than just your appearance" — as important as that is to teens. If your teen fights that reassurance, the best thing to do is back off so he or she doesn't fight it more.

Pearl 2

❖

Aggressive Behavior

Bill and Alice always had been proud of their son Billy. As a child, he grew like a weed, ate like a horse, and appeared to be a natural leader. Billy played sports aggressively and won the respect of his playmates—or so Bill and Alice thought.

By the time Billy turned twelve, he was taller than Alice. At fifteen, he towered above Bill. His younger brother and sister cowered around him, especially when he was angry—which was most of the time. Billy was stronger than all of them put together, and he knew it.

Billy had already earned a reputation at school as an antisocial bully. Now he took his aggressiveness out on his family. He learned that he could ignore his parents when it suited him. He treated simple chores such as taking out the trash or raking the yard as big productions, and he made sure that Bill and Alice knew it in no uncertain terms.

When Bill or Alice confronted Billy about his unwillingness to do chores, he would just as soon flip them off as ignore them.

By age sixteen, Billy turned abusive—verbally as well as physically. When his frustrated parents yelled at him to straighten up, Billy screamed back a string of profanities.

159

Then he started pushing his mother away and shoving his father up against the wall. To make a point, Billy also threw plates and even furniture.

This was no ordinary disrespect. This was violence by a child against his family.

At first, Bill tried to reason with Billy. He chose to talk to him when family matters were quiet, and said, "Son, we know that adolescence is a tough time, but you have no right to treat your mother that way."

"Shove it, Dad. I'm sick of your bull."

Bill dropped the conversation there.

He and Alice then found a family counselor who was willing to meet with them and Billy and talk it over.

Billy would have none of it. "I'm not wasting my time to talk to a d — - shrink!" he shouted, slamming around whatever was close at hand to drive home his point.

So Bill and Alice had a decision to make. Although it was painful decision, they made the right one.

They gave Billy the choice of enrolling in a military academy or finding a place to live where his behavior would be more accepted. Either way, they no longer permitted him to live at home.

Billy chose to live on the street.

Bill and Alice told him that they loved him and would consider admitting him to the household again if he decided to change his ways and seek counseling. But until such time, they told him that he was not permitted inside the house, and if he tried to violate that rule they would call the police.

Parents rarely face such a hard choice. It is a shattered dream. Bill and Alice didn't do this because they were mean or selfish. They did it to protect themselves and their other children from physical harm. Their concern for Billy had to be balanced with their need to ensure family safety and protection.

Pearl 3

❖

APPEARANCE: CLOTHING, HAIRSTYLE, AND OTHER SURPRISES

In adolescence, for better or worse, children show their autonomy and independence from adults by their appearance. Actually, considering all the *other* ways kids can show autonomy and independence, most appearance issues are really fairly harmless. It's not worth the trouble to engage in control battles over them.

We all like to know that we "fit" within one group or another. Teens are no different.

CLOTHES AND THE NEED TO FIT IN

I (Foster) remember when, long ago, as a younger parent, I would find out that "weird" meant "different," and "different" meant "special," and "special" meant "awesome" — as long as the "in group" dressed different, special, and awesome.

One morning, as I waited to drive my eighth-grade daughter to school, she came down dressed like a cheerleader — in a short, flouncy dress that barely reached to mid-thigh. Had she been a cheerleader going to practice, this would have been wonderful.

Now don't get me wrong — for the most part, I am a

fairly "easy" dad. Nevertheless, even *I* could not think of any real good reason for her to walk into school in a dress that looked like it had come to a bad end in the dryer. By that time in my parenting career, however, I had learned that the first things I tend to say are often wrong. So if Dad says anything, Dad gives it some thought first.

After mulling over various possibilities on the way to school, I said, "Robin, have you given the way you dress a lot of thought? I'm wondering if you set yourself up as being a little different when you dress like that?"

She smiled at me and quickly replied, "Oh, Dad, all the girls dress like this."

I thought, *I'm sure. All the girls!? No pants? Give me a break!* But, luckily, I kept my mouth closed.

When we got to school, we pulled up behind all the buses with their red lights flashing, students streaming out of them. I noticed with a shock that *all* the girls wore cheerleader outfits — but they weren't cheerleaders! Again I learned that my child often knew what she was talking about. Yet no matter how often I learned that, it always came as a surprise.

CLOTHES AND THE NEED TO STAND OUT

Teens' desire to fit in with their peers is often at odds with what adults think is "normal" dress. Paradoxically, teens struggle with the need to fit in at the same time they're struggling with the need to stand out.

Teens will sometimes go to great lengths to make their exterior unavoidably apparent. Why would anyone who wants to be accepted dress so unacceptably, we wonder? The answer is fairly easy. The teen reasons, "If anyone accepts me, they'll have to accept the real me — and they'll have to handle or ignore the way I look!"

Parents regrettably undermine their teen's self-respect when they insist that they look "normal," even though what's "normal" changes from year to year.

For example, when you go to Aunt Hilda's funeral and you're about to see all these family members you haven't seen in a while—and you know everybody's judging how well your family has turned out—you show up with your teenage girl who, in your eyes, looks like a fright. You want to tell her, "Why can't you, just this one time, put on a regular dress and comb your hair nicely. What's wrong with looking normal?"

But using the phrase "look normal" is very devastating to a teenager. To get your point across without alienating your daughter, you might say instead, "If you go dressed like that, luckily for me, I know what a neat kid you are. I don't judge you by how you look. But there will be a few relatives there who will probably stay on the other side of the coffin. So please give it some thought." That way, your daughter knows that what she wears reflects on her, not you.

Also, teens may dress atrociously as a statement of identity. "I am not my dad or mom! Since my parents can't stand the way I look, this has to be the real me, because I know I'm different from them!" Teens create their own identities by imitating the styles of their athletic, music, or media heroes, and in turn adapt them to their own bodies.

HAIRSTYLE, MAKEUP, AND EARRINGS

The same holds true for hairstyles. Teens have expressed their personalities by their hairstyles with flattops in the fifties, afros and long hair in the sixties, punk cuts in the seventies, and the intricate razor cuts in recent years. Parents can't control what a hairstylist will do to their teens' heads. If Mom or Dad really disapproves of how their teens wear their hair, they can refuse to pay the extra money it might cost for a new style.

Makeup can be a problem issue, too. The age at which

girls use makeup largely depends on where they live and the value system in their peer group. Usually, most girls start wearing makeup when they're in junior high school. The rule of thumb for appearance in general and makeup in particular is not to let your girl stick out like a sore thumb. Some parents can unconsciously set their daughters up to be socially isolated, however, by forbidding them to wear makeup when it's a common practice among their peers.

Even more problematic than makeup on girls is earrings on boys. In the past decade, increasing numbers of young men have shocked their parents by piercing their ears. This style was once considered a fashion statement by homosexual men, but that identification has faded. If parents find a pierced ear on their teenage son objectionable, they can ask that he not wear the earring in the house.

Sometimes a teen's attire and apparent rebelliousness reflects what he sees at home rather than what he sees on television or in school.

Donald Sr., a well-known and well-respected lawyer, came to see me because he was upset about the way Don Jr. dressed. "The way that kid dresses, nobody's going to want to see hide nor hair of him, let alone hire him," groused Don Sr.

One day I saw Don Sr. at the courthouse and was somewhat shocked to see him wearing jeans (albeit nice jeans) with a white shirt and tie. I questioned him, with some surprise, about the way he was dressed. "Well, I'm just here in court doin' my thing," Donald Sr. said. "If people don't like the way I'm dressed, that's their problem. I think they can figure out that I know my stuff."

No wonder Don Jr. was rebellious about his attire!

THREE RULES OF THUMB

Here are some suggestions for handling an adolescent's appearance:

1. *If you can, say something nice.* If it isn't stretching the truth too much, comment favorably on almost every change in dress or haircut that your child chooses. This has one great advantage: If your teen is very rebellious, it might drive him or her back to an appearance that's more to your liking.
2. *If you can't say something nice, don't say anything.* If it's stretching the truth too much to make a positive comment, then mum's the word.
3. *If it's offensive, draw your own line.* If your teen's appearance is completely beyond the laws of decorum and good taste, you can simply say, "I know you appreciate that style of dress, but it is beyond my limits and I don't want you to be dressed like that when you're with me. I'm a little old-fashioned, as are most of my friends, and unfortunately we have our limits."

In summary, above all, try to avoid control battles over appearance. Schools and parents have lost plenty of those conflicts. Give yourself a break.

Pearl 4

❖

ARGUMENTS

Raising teens is a risky business. No matter how parents play most situations, they are still risky. You are about to read a conversation between a basically responsible teen and a very loving mother. Before rejecting this mother's response as uncaring, unsympathetic, or dangerous, it must be remembered that prohibiting a child to sell drugs has a track record of *not* working.

Many drug dealers have disappointed parents who ordered their children, when younger, to stop all sorts of antisocial and negative behavior. Such orders are simply not effective. It must be kept in mind that Mark is a basically responsible youth. If Mark were basically irresponsible the approach would have to be modified. Notice how this wise, love-and-logic mom keeps her cool and avoids a major-league argument.

> MARK: "Okay, if you guys don't love me enough to give me more allowance, I'll just have to start selling drugs!"
>
> MOM: "Well, I guess that's an option."
>
> MARK: "That's an option? What do you mean *that's an option*?"

MOM (shrugs): "That could be one way to solve your problem."

MARK: "You've got to be crazy! What's wrong with you?"

MOM: "Nothing. Even though I love you more than anything in the world, the time has come when you have to decide for yourself how you are going to live your life."

MARK: "No way. You're on something. Otherwise you'd be giving me a lot of grief about this! Do you know that I could get caught for dealing? I could go to jail!"

MOM: "True. But maybe you'll make enough money dealing that you can hire some good lawyers to get you some light time. I'm sure you've thought it all out. Anyway, just think, if you get caught, the state will take care of you. You won't have to worry about allowance, room and board, or anything."

MARK: "Wait a minute! How am I supposed to go to college?"

MOM (relaxed, reclining on the couch): "Oh, you won't be in the slammer forever. With good behavior you'll get out and go to college later. You might even be better prepared because you'll have more life experiences."

MARK: "This is weird, man! Are you just going to sit there and let me *ruin my life*? Don't you even care about what happens to me? I can't listen to this!" (Stomps out of the room.)

As farfetched as this sounds, it is an actual conversation with a parent who had learned to keep the monkey on the back of the teen who owned the problem. She had learned that teens love to "hit" us, like Mark did in this situation.

Mark hoped to engage his mom in defending herself and making demands on him. When teens such as Mark are successful at getting this far, then they switch into their judge role with statements such as "That's not fair" or "I can't do that." Before long the parent totally owns a problem the teen actually needs to learn to solve.

But Mom did not criticize Mark's thinking by saying, "That's stupid. Don't you dare do that!" Nor did she tell him what to do with a comment like, "If you want to go to that concert badly enough, you'll go out and get yourself an honest job." And Mom did not use anger, guilt, intimidation, or orders such as, "As long as you live in my house you're not going to talk like that!"

Mom remembered that the magic response, "That's an option," will apply regardless of the brilliance or foolishness of a teen's suggestion. She refused to take Mark's bait by doing his thinking for him and ultimately taking over ownership of his problem.

The second skill Mom used was to think of all the advantages to Mark's solution of selling drugs. However, she stated them in negative—yet enthusiastic—terms. As you can tell from the dialogue, it blew Mark's mind. So he switched into the role of telling *her* what was wrong with dealing drugs.

The third thing Mom knew was that Mark could learn from this type of dialogue because she had a reasonably good relationship with him and things had gone well during his childhood.

Clear thinking and calm emotions go far in defusing otherwise explosive arguments. And remember, if you lose your cool the first time you apply these love-and-logic principles, you can count on your teen to give you another opportunity to practice. Take heart!

Pearl 5

❖

BACK IN THE NEST: IF AN OLDER CHILD NEEDS TO MOVE HOME

"Mom, can I come home?"

For some parents, this question was once a plea from a teenager who had strayed, recognized the dead-end of that lifestyle, and wanted to make a new start.

Today, for many parents, this question is often a cry for economic rescue. And parents are often caught in the middle between their child's plight and their own needs.

Increasing numbers of young people in their late teens to mid-twenties are going through the experience of losing a job or splitting up with a spouse. They only way they can make ends meet after such financial hardships is to move in with their parents—even if they had just moved out only a few years before.

Parents often want to help. But they should keep a few things in mind.

First, *the primary rule when older children want to move home is that parents now wear two hats—parent and landlord.* Parents should require whatever a landlord would require, but perhaps not as strictly.

Second, *adult children need to have an appropriately thankful attitude for the opportunity to return home.* Parents need to be grateful, too—yet firm! However, home is not a place for the child to come and "hang out." After all, a landlord doesn't allow people to "hang out" at property he owns.

You can say, "I know what a good deal it is for you to be here. Now, I want you to tell me what benefits are in this for me?"

You hope your grownup child will say, "I'll do the laundry"; "I'll mow the lawn"; "I'll paint the garage." If he or she doesn't, then you must decide whether you should allow your child to stay with you.

The bottom line: If it's not a win-win situation, it's a lose-lose situation. It's a two-way street or it's a no-way street.

Pearl 6

❖

BACKTALK

"This stinks!"

It probably does. The question for you as a parent, however, is how you deal with your teen's backtalk.

There are three possible reasons why adolescents mouth off to us:

1. They backtalk because we are threatening their autonomy and independence.

2. They backtalk because they, like the rest of us, have the inalienable right to protest.

3. Backtalk may be a part of other issues, including poor school behavior, use of drugs, mood swings, or basic irresponsibility.

THE THREAT TO THEIR INDEPENDENCE

The first reason is the healthiest and easiest to deal with. If your child was a basically good and loving child through the fifth or sixth grade, then almost certainly you can help you child clean up the backtalk.

First, *listen to your child's ideas.*

Second *offer your ideas without trying to make your child do it your way.*

If you have had a good relationship with your children, they will love and respect you and realize that you are usually right.

Our children will test us to see whether or not we will rescue them by feeling sorry for them when they talk back to us. But after they find out that we continue in a loving way to give our point of view, refuse to rescue, and — without being angry — allow them to suffer the consequences of their behavior, they will stop most of their backtalk.

Here's a scenario showing how a parent can deal with this first category of backtalk. This dad has picked a moment when his daughter is in a relatively good mood. He mainly asks questions; he doesn't lecture. And he starts out by focusing on Sarah's feelings, not on her backtalk or tacky behavior. He knows that teens need to be understood before they are willing to talk about actions.

> DAD: "Sarah, sometimes you and I have a pretty hard time together. I would really appreciate our talking about that for a few minutes. What do you think the problem could be?"
>
> SARAH: "You're always on my case."
>
> DAD: "Like how?"
>
> SARAH: "Like everything. You try to choose my friends and tell me what I have to do all the time. *Everything.*"
>
> DAD: "Then how do you feel?"
>
> SARAH: "Like nuthin' I do is right."
>
> DAD: "And then how do you act toward me?"
>
> SARAH: "I get mad, Dad."
>
> DAD: "I know you do. I've been realizing, Sarah, that I've been always trying to make sure you do the right thing and see that you don't get in trouble. I've been trying to help you live a happy life. I realize that I'm not giving you the right to make your own mistakes. And I just want to apologize.

Everyone has the right to make mistakes. I'm sorry Sarah."

SARAH (stunned): "Well—that's okay, Dad."

DAD: "No, it isn't okay. It robs you of deciding for yourself when you come in or how important school is."

SARAH: "Well, you *should* worry about some things. Like maybe I do drink too much at a few parties."

DAD: "I know. But that may not be a real big deal. Of course, if I think you're drinking and driving, I'll just give the license plate number to the cops. No big deal. And if you've had too much to drink, don't come home until you're sober. I have trouble handling anyone around the house who has had too much to drink, so don't take it personally."

SARAH: "Dad, get serious!"

DAD: "I am serious. I love you too much to keep messing around trying to save you and make sure everything goes okay. Thanks for talking."

SARAH (doubtfully): "Thanks—I guess."

THE RIGHT TO PROTEST

When you're dealing with backtalk, remember that all of us—including our children—have the right to protest. We may not like paying taxes, and we may gripe, but we pay them. When we accept our children's protest, they usually feel understood—and that's often enough to satisy their need, so they don't have to up the ante to outright disrespect.

Here's an example of how to handle the second type of backtalk situation:

MOM: "Jason, would you please empty the trash?"

JASON: "I hate emptying the trash. I do everything around here."

MOM: "I know, honey. It's a bummer when there are always jobs to do. Thanks for doing it anyway."

This smart parent was thanking the child in advance. It works with "Thanks for not smoking" signs in public places and it may work for your child. Society oftens thanks us for our cooperation before we actually give it!

Humor can often defuse backtalk or even disrespect. Sometimes when a child makes a common obscene comment, we can simply say, "Richard, you always have sex on your mind."

If teens' backtalk and disrespect is extreme, it is sometimes best simply to let them know that they may need to leave and come back when they can talk differently. The wise parent says, "I'm having trouble listening to this," rather than, "Don't you dare talk that way to me!"

WHEN BACKTALK IS PART OF A BIGGER PROBLEM

When backtalk is part of a bigger problem, such as a symptom of drug abuse or poor school behavior, it requires a much firmer tack. Instead of allowing more freedom with its consequences, parental structure may need to be tightened. Consequences may need to be imposed, rather than simply being allowed to occur. These problems are deeper than just establishing independence or protesting. It is usually best to confer with a professional before attempting to deal with these serious issues.

In summary, if backtalk starts in adolescence, it is almost always because we have not allowed the child enough opportunity to suffer and learn from mistakes. Teens who backtalk often have parents who get angry and then rescue the child from the results of their mistakes. This is known as the "3-R parenting style" — rant, rave, and rescue. It is almost guaranteed to bring the worst out of a teen.

Pearl 7

❖

CARS, DRIVING, AND CATCHING RIDES

Teenage transportation is a thought-provoking issue for parents. All we have to do is imagine other teens driving our kids around, or our kids driving themselves and their friends around, and plenty of thoughts will come to mind.

We want to handle car responsibilities with our teens the way the real world does. Having wheels is a great privilege as well as a great responsibility.

Before teens learn to drive, we should explore with them the new dangers they're going to face. Some parents handle the transportation issue by laying down the law. Other parents handle it by getting their teens to think about life in the fast lane. Effective parents might hold a conversation like this:

> DAD: "Kyle, if you were to die before you were twenty-one—and I hope you don't—how, statistically, would you die?"
>
> KYLE: "I don't know."
>
> DAD: "Oh, I bet you do. What are the two major ways teens die?"
>
> KYLE: "Suicide?"
>
> DAD: "Right. Do you think you're the suicidal type?"

KYLE: "No. . . ."

DAD: "I don't either. So you probably won't die by suicide. How else would you die early?"

KYLE: "Car accident?"

DAD: "Right! If you were to die before you were twenty-one, it would probably be in a car accident. And generally, in these car accidents, there is something else involved. What's that?"

KYLE: "Alcohol."

DAD: "You're right. Do you think about this very often, or don't you think about it much?"

KYLE: "I don't think about it much."

DAD: "I see. Now, considering the kids who die, do you think they think about it a lot, or do you think they probably don't?"

KYLE: "They probably don't."

DAD: "Right. So you fit the profile. Anyway, I just want you to know that I love you and would miss you if you were killed before you're twenty-one."

KYLE: "I know, Dad. I'll be careful."

DAD: "Thanks."

This love-and-logic dad has placed the responsibility of driving squarely in Kyle's lap. He guides his son in realizing that driving is a life-and-death issue, but he doesn't threaten or cajole him. Future conversations along these lines can help Kyle spell out how he will be careful in other driving situations.

There are other general love-and-logic strategies for handling teenage transportation issues.

First, *wise parents consider offering their teens "good guy" auto insurance.* "Good guy" auto insurance means the parents pay the premium based on teens maintaining a "B" average in school, achieving a flawless driving record, and in most states, having completed driver's education. Then, if teens get a ticket or their grades slide down, parents can respond with sorrow, not anger, as they say, "Gee, what a bummer for you. Your insurance is going to go up now. How do you think you'll pay for the increase?"

Second, *wise parents do not buy cars for their teens unless their teens are responsible, nose-to-the grindstone young adults.* Many teens own their own cars—and many more *want* to. In most cases, the parents are the ones who buy them. However, we believe that parents should buy a car for their teen only if the teen has demonstrated that he or she can handle the responsibility. And then, the car they buy should be an old one. If the teen has an accident, the parents don't have to get bent out of shape—only the car is bent out of shape.

Third, *parents have the right to restrict who rides with their teen when the teen is driving.* After all, it's their car. However, parents ought to set reasonable restrictions by carefully explaining why certain people should not ride with their teens.

Finally, a word of caution. Most states allow teens to get their driver's license when they have reached age sixteen. However, many teens who are chronologically sixteen are socially and emotionally age fourteen or younger. Some children, who may have repeated several grades, are still in junior high school at sixteen. Wise parents will discourage their teens from obtaining a license until they are socially and emotionally sixteen years of age. Generally speaking, this means the teen is functioning on an eleventh-grade level.

I (Jim) am a strong advocate for teens making a deposit in the parents' savings account, equal to the amount of the insurance deductible, prior to driving. The parent-teen understanding is that in the event of an accident the money will go to repair the car. The youngster will then be able to drive again once a new deposit is made. Teens who drive under these conditions are usually much safer drivers. Here's a sample conversation between Mom and teen on car insurance.

TAMMY: "Mom, am I going to get to use the family car when I get my driver's license?"

MOM: "Sure. All you'll need to do is make a deposit in my savings account for the amount of the insurance deductible: $250."

TAMMY: "How come?"

MOM: "That way if you're unfortunate enough to have an accident, I won't have to worry about getting the car fixed."

TAMMY: "I don't have that much money."

MOM: "Oh, I might consider holding something of yours for the deposit as long as it's valuable enough for me to sell quickly to get the $250. Or maybe you'd like to call the agent and do some cost comparisons on lowering the deductible? Then you could make up the difference in the premiums. Either is fine with me."

Tammy makes a call to the agent and comes back for another talk with Mom.

TAMMY: "Geez, Mom, if we lower the deductible, the premiums go out of sight. I can't afford that."

MOM: "Now you know why we have a higher deductible. What are you going to do?"

TAMMY: "If I let you hold some of my stuff, do I still get to use it?"

MOM: "No, banks don't operate that way."

TAMMY: "Well, what happens if I have an accident and you sell my stuff to pay the deductible? Do I still get to drive?"

MOM: "Oh, you'll get to drive again as soon as you come up with another deposit. But don't worry about it, I'm sure you'll be careful. Let me know when you've decided what you're going to do."

Pearl 8

❖

COLLEGE EXPENSES: WHO PAYS?

One of the best gifts we can give our teens is an education. If God has given us enough resources to help them obtain a college education, we should do it. The development of the mind is something permanent that we can do for our children, because neither hard economic times nor physical illness can take away an education.

But like all gifts and privileges, a college education can be abused. Teenagers are much more prone to be careless and drop out when someone else is paying for it.

Colleges themselves can abuse the education process because it's better for them financially if students take five or six years instead of four to graduate. Sometimes, the encouragement subtly creeps in for students to meander through school and "find themselves." The question is, whose dime is that done on?

Sometimes parents will fall into the trap of paying for college to "encourage" teens, falsely reasoning, "If I don't pay, he'll never get an education." Teens, of course, will use that argument, too, to hook Mom and Dad into a guilt trip: "If you don't shell out for tuition, room and board, and books for Behemoth U., I'll have to beg for a living, and then what will your friends say?"

In twenty years of working with children, I (Foster) have never seen a teen flunk out of college on his or her own dime. Allowing your son or daughter to finance a college education is one of the best (and last!) ways you can teach your teen fiscal and intellectual responsibility.

There are several options parents and their teens can use to pay for college:

1. Parents can pay a percentage of college expenses, from none of them to all of them.
2. The more responsible the teenager, the safer it is for parents to pay the whole bill.
3. The safest plan is for parents to tell teens, "You pay for the first semester of college. After you get through the first semester, send me a report card with average or above average grades, and then I'll reimburse you so you can pay for the second semester."
4. Some wise parents say, "I will pay for four years of undergraduate State U. tuition. If you want to go out of state, fine: I'll pay the same amount as in-state tuition, and you pay for the difference."
5. Some teens are really industrious and want to help pay for their own tuition, room and board, and books by working at often low-paying jobs. Their parents may want to reward their industriousness by matching their wages on a percentage basis to be agreed upon by the teens and their parents.

Regardless of the financial plan you agree upon, remember that college is the final transition from childhood to adulthood for teens. You can help them on their journey (and even inspire them to study harder!) by discussing their classes, ideas, and adventures with them. This will help you monitor their progress while you build the kind of friendship you want to have with your adult children.

Pearl 9

❖

CRISIS SITUATIONS

A car wreck. A drug overdose. A suicide. A runaway teen.

Families struggle with the different kinds of crises, but each and every one carries its own unique trauma and pain. When a crisis hits our lives or the lives of our teens, it can send us reeling. Guilt, worry, anxiety, anger, and inconsolable grief are some of the emotions that can stagger us.

When a crisis hits, the first thing to remember is, *Don't panic*. Most of us think that something has to be done RIGHT NOW. This is seldom true. The Chinese language has an intriguing character for crisis, combining the symbols for danger and opportunity. We see the danger all too well, but we often miss the opportunity.

Use these four thoughts to help you deal with a crisis:

1. Crises, by their very nature, are generally temporary. Knowing that better times lie ahead can help you guard against overinvolvement and overreaction.
2. Almost no crisis must be dealt with immediately. You will usually have time to pray and think and act rationally.
3. Cope with the "what if's" by asking yourself what

the worst possible outcome of the crisis would be. Often, you'll find that you can actually cope with that.

4. As much as you can, keep the monkey on the back of the person(s) responsible for the problems related to the crisis.

The knowledge that every crisis is temporary helps us to avoid becoming overinvolved. Generally, in every crisis there is time to seek advice from others who have had similar experiences or who are professionally capable of dealing with the situation.

Sometimes, what we might perceive as a crisis is certainly a serious issue but not really a crisis. The problem — such as illicit sexual activity, a life-threatening illness, or drug use — may have been going on for months or years. *Then* it comes to the attention of the parents, and *that's what makes it a crisis!* Sometimes we need to stop and evaluate whether the situation is really a crisis in order to decide how to respond appropriately.

You may find it helpful to ask yourself, "What would happen if I did nothing at all?" That may not be a good solution, but it might clarify things enough so that you'll get a better idea of what you *are* able to do. When you're up against a crisis, don't just react — first, sit down and write out all your options. Then talk over those options with a person you respect.

Good resources at this time are people you respect at your church, school, county social services, or friends and neighbors who have a good track record with raising their own children. Many local sheriff's offices have a chaplain. They are familiar with the resources available.

Don't pass up this opportunity to solidify your relationship with your teen. We often get some great help and understanding from teens when we ask, "How can I best help you through this?"

The appealing thing about acting hastily is that you can almost always "do something." But once you "do something" — like moving a person with a broken back — it may be difficult to undo what you've done. What's more important is doing the *right thing* — not just *something*.

A general rule is that the more sincere questions a parent asks, the better the results. The more orders, accusations, and demands, the worse we mess up the situation.

Finally, it's important that you acknowledge the worst possible outcome. Often, that outcome is simply death. Once you look it in the face, you won't be spending valuable energy trying to deny that possibility. The acceptance will free you up to focus your energies in positive directions. Keep the faith — it's your best weapon.

Pearl 10

❖

CURFEWS

The real world doesn't have curfews, except during civil emergencies. If we're raising our teens to live in the real world, we shouldn't have curfews, either. Instead, we should negotiate when they will come home.

I (Jim) remember how we negotiated with our teenagers. We would start when they were thirteen and ask, "Where are you going to be? How long? Is that enough time? Can you get home by then? Will you let us know if it's a problem?" We continued negotiating with them as they got older.

The rule in our household is: "We'll know where you are and you'll know where we are. So if we go away, we'll let you know. If there's an emergency, we always want to be able to get in touch with you. You need to be able to contact us."

That worked pretty well until I came home two hours late one night, and Charlie started yelling at me that he'd been worrying about me for two hours. Then I found out that it was a two-way street.

I (Foster) didn't have firm curfews with my kids, either. We'd say, "What time do you expect to be home?"

My son would respond, "Well, the dance is over at

twelve p.m., and we may go out to get something to eat afterwards. I'll be home at one a.m."

"Well, if you're not going to be home at one, will you phone?"

"Yes."

Later, we'd have to make sure that when he did phone us, we didn't say, "Now look, you said you were going to be home at one." Then he'd never phone again. Instead, we took a deep breath and said, "Gee, thanks for phoning. What are the new plans?"

"We're popping corn at Jeanne's."

"Is that all you're popping?"

"Yes, Dad!"

"Thank you. Okay, just checking. Now, when do you think you'll be home?"

"Well, we thought we'd stay here another hour, and then we'll be home."

"Okay. Thanks."

I (Jim) had to be up front with my teens when they came in late and say, "You didn't get home on time. I missed a lot of sleep. I was really concerned for you. We'll talk about it another time." Then I went off to bed. I would keep my mouth shut until the next time they said they were going to go out, then I would say, "Oh, gee, I'm just not up to worrying tonight. Why don't you stick around?" Or, "I'm sorry. You can't go out tonight, honey. I need my sleep."

When teenagers don't come home at a reasonable hour, most parents react first by getting scared and then by getting angry. We can't do anything by getting scared, so we get mad. But in this case, anger is an ineffective emotion.

If we can show our teenagers that their coming home late frightens us, it will have more power and impact than our anger. We don't want to worry—that's why we would appreciate knowing where they are and hearing from them by phone when they're late. We want them to come home when they're supposed to — whatever the agreed-upon time.

Here's a conversation in which a love-and-logic parent helps her teen see that phoning home if she's going to be late is a sensible agreement:

> MOM: "We're not the type of parents who are always worrying. Let's say you're supposed to be home by midnight, but you show up at two a.m. instead. If we don't have an agreement that you will call to tell us where you are and how much later you're going to be, we'll just figure that you're out there somewhere, doing fine. But you could be lying beside the road. And fifteen minutes could be the difference in saving your life."
>
> BRITTANY: "Gee, Mom, don't make it sound so dramatic. I'm not going out to look for trouble and wind up in a gang fight."
>
> MOM: "I didn't think so. You see, if we have an agreement that you will give me a phone call if you're going to be later than you're supposed to be, then I know what to do when twelve-thirty rolls around and you were supposed to be in by midnight but you haven't called. I'll phone the police and tell them, 'I'm not an overprotective parent. My kid is always responsible about phoning. This is the license plate on her car. She's in trouble somewhere.' Then I can get you help real quick."
>
> BRITTANY: "Well, that seems reasonable. But why make such a big deal about it?"
>
> MOM: "Because if we make a decision that you can come in anytime and you're not going to phone me when you're late, then my decision is to figure that you're probably okay somewhere. Maybe you're not — but you won't be getting any help. So give it some thought."
>
> BRITTANY: "Okay, I can live with that."

We can put faith in people to act in their own best interests. We act on this faith when we say, "If you operate in this way, your life is likely to be more happy. So please give it some thought."

We're often most effective when we simply let our teens know what our concerns are. After we talk them out we can say, "I really hope you'll let me know. I hope this doesn't happen again, because I think it stresses our relationship. And you're way ahead if our relationship is good. I think that when you do things that stress me out a lot, it doesn't work out well for you in the long run, sweetheart. So I hope you give these things some thought."

Pearl 11

---❖---

DATING

Jennifer's parents were proud of her. Jennifer was in the ninth grade, but she was so mentally advanced for her age that she was taking eleventh grade math.

Math wasn't the only thing that Jennifer liked. She was maturing physically and liked the guys. Several juniors had already asked her out.

Her parents didn't feel the same way about junior guys. They firmly said no, telling her, "Well, you're not *that* mature."

Jennifer and her mom couldn't resolve the issue, so they came to me (Foster) for advice. Mom stood her ground and stated flatly that no way would her daughter date boys two years older than she was.

Jennifer wailed, "Mom, if you knew those ninth grade boys, you wouldn't want to date them either."

There is no hard and fast "right" age to begin dating, nor is there an appropriate limit to the age difference between your teen and the teen he or she wants to date.

Such "rules" about dating, like most other "rules," create their own problems. As soon as you come up with a hard and fast rule, your teen will bring up an exception to that rule. In turn, dating becomes another control battle that the parent will lose — and consequently lose respect in the eyes of the child.

For example, Gretchen's mom told her that she was forbidden to date that no-good biker, Bill. So as far as her mom knew Gretchen never dated Bill — but because Gretchen's every move could not be monitored, Bill did become the father of her baby. Gretchen's mom was unwise to ignore Gretchen's emerging independence.

We might think it's hard to avoid such rules like the ones Gretchen's mom set for her, especially when our children are about to begin dating. We've been used to our children's behavior within our families and with their friends. But now dating comes along and seems to be the springboard that launches our children into adolescence and adulthood as they interact with the opposite sex. We worry about them taking the plunge.

We should be excited for our teens at this time. It helps to remember that girls and boys mature at different rates. Although there are exceptions, girls such as Jennifer mature earlier than boys and usually begin dating earlier than boys, too. We can invite our teens to talk to us about kids they're interested in or about who's interested in them. But we should cut them some slack if they don't want to talk about dating.

Inevitably, some dates are diamonds, and some dates are stones. Teens' egos tend to be fragile at this time, especially in boys when girls turn them down for dates. We need to befriend our children when they go through times that seem overwhelmingly traumatic.

Discuss with your teens who they will date, the activities they will engage in, and the hours they will keep. You might want to offer some suggestions for activities. After all, you dated once, too! These discussions can go a long way in enhancing your friendship with your teens.

One of the most important things you can do about your teen's dating is to know who your teen's friends are. Show interest in your teen's friends, even if you don't approve of everything about them. After all, you wouldn't want your teen to judge *your* friends.

Have faith in your parenting that you've taught your child some lessons about how to make decisions. And have faith in your child to make the right decisions and live with the consequences.

A girl once told me (Foster), "Up until midnight, I'm a princess. But at one minute past twelve, I turn into a pumpkin." Her parents, ordering her to "Be back at midnight and not one minute later!" had not yet learned to have faith in their daughter or her ability to make decisions.

We shouldn't jump to the assumption that an otherwise responsible son or daughter will act irresponsibly while dating. On the other hand, it's foolish to assume that an irresponsible teen will behave responsibly.

Those assumptions about teens' responsibilities (or lack of them) in dating hit closest to home when parents deal with their teens' dating and possible sexual activity. Parents like to warn their teens of all the dangers of premarital intimacy. But parents need to realize that behind every warning lies a hidden expectation.

Wise parents don't send the message to their children that they will engage in early sex by saying something irresponsible like, "You better watch out! Your emotions will get the best of you and before you know it you'll have sex." Such a pessimistic comment appears to make sexually responsible behavior nearly impossible for teens. So if they engage in sex, teens will then reason, it's something they couldn't help.

Much better is for parents to share clearly both good sexual values as well as basic information. You might say, "Dating and intimacy can lead to sexual involvement. Before you take such a step, you need to decide for yourself if having sex before marriage is a wise choice. You already know how I feel about that. But if it does happen I'm sure you will talk to me about it, act responsibly, and accept the consequences of your decision." Such a discussion shows your teen that you're not as ignorant about his or her behavior as your teen might assume. It also fosters mutual respect between parents and teens.

Keep discussions matter-of-fact. With responsible teens, we don't have to elaborate on what the consequences of a pregnancy might be. With irresponsible teens, however, we must ask appropriate questions: "How would you pay for an obstetrician?" "How would you care for a baby?" "What kind of job would you get to support a family?" These are not flippant questions. They have lifelong implications.

If your teen has not yet shown that he or she is responsible, you need to bring a jolt of reality by telling him or her that dating could be a rough road. You might say, "This is a two-generation home, where parents and children live; not a three-generation home of parents, children, and grandchildren. This is not a group home for children." For most teens, that's a nice way of saying, "If you have children, they won't live here," and communicating the expectation that teens will make good choices and conduct themselves responsibly.

Since there is no hard-and-fast rule about when a teen is old enough to date, our emphasis should be on the teen's decision making. A teen is ready when he or she can describe a plan for handling the situations that concern the parent.

Pearl 12

❖

DISRESPECT

Sometimes our teens' problems become our problems as well. These problems often revolve around the issue of their disrespect for us.

But in order to gain our teens' respect, we must first learn to respect ourselves.

One of my (Jim's) friends had teenagers who were just impossible. She told me, "I couldn't drive anywhere without them hanging out the windows, yelling at other motorists, telling other people how to drive, flipping the bird, the whole works. It was so embarrassing, I couldn't stand it."

She resolved the problem by applying love-and-logic principles — first, to herself. The next time her teens started acting up, she pulled over, got out of the car, and said, "Okay everybody. *Out.*"

But she had a problem with this order. She was staring at two teenagers twice her size who responded, "No way. You can't make us get out." And she thought to herself, *At this point, they're right.*

Like all good consultant parents, she started to buy time. In other words, she started backpedaling. The first thing she said was, "Did I forget to ask in a nice way?"

They said, "You asked in a nice way."

She said, "And you're not going to do it?"

And they said, "No way. You can't make us get out."

"Oh boy, I thought it would work."

"It won't work on us."

"Well, I'd better think this over."

"Yeah, you'd better think it over a whole bunch."

"Would you guys mind if I walked across the street to that restaurant and got a cup of coffee while I'm thinking this over?"

And these smart-alecky teens said, "Mom, whatever turns you on. You've just got to go for it."

So she said, "Thank you," and walked across the street.

They immediately started playing their radios, having a wonderful time to show her that it didn't bother them. After a while, they noticed she'd been gone fifteen minutes, then twenty minutes. Pretty soon they were saying, "Wait a minute! What's going on here?"

Suddenly something very strange happened across the street. Mom's best friend drove up to the front of the restaurant. Mom came out, got in the car, and off she went with a little wave on the way.

This mom later recalled that she thought they would be madder than hornets when they got home. But she was ready for them. She watched them get out of the taxi and walk to the front door. When they walked in, they did not say one word. Months went by, and they never said a word. She thinks they'll bring it up at some family reunion. "Oh, Mom, remember that day you ditched us?"

This mom gained respect. How? By taking good care of herself first. "The bigger my kids get, the more I have to fall back on that," she said.

"Up until that day, I was a doormat for them. They wiped their feet on me all the time. They had no respect whatsoever. I used to beg for it. I used to demand it. I used to yell at my husband, *What are you going to do to make those kids show me some respect?*"

"I finally discovered something. You never ever get respect by demanding or pleading for it. You get respect when you start treating yourself with respect."

And you know what her teens had been saying to themselves all that time? "Well, it's my mom, and she knows herself better than anybody else. She knows whether or not she deserves any respect." They now say, "My mom knows herself better than anybody else. She knows she deserves respect."

"Life is a whole lot better just after that one time," this mom reflected. "We don't have to do it over and over. Isn't that funny? The consequences of winning respect came like a bolt out of the blue — with no anger, with no lectures, and with words at a minimum. I feel a whole lot more powerful now than I ever did before because I'm learning how to take care of myself. I used to think it would hurt my kids if I did that. But I'm finding out that they're more capable and fun to be around."

Teens' respect for their parents is a critical issue for how families function. But paradoxically, we win other's respect only after we demonstrate respect for ourselves first.

In extreme cases when disrespectful teens refuse to change no matter how much we model respect for ourselves, we may want to seek professional help. But for most conflicts, our self-respect will cancel out our teens' disrespect.

Pearl 13

❖

DRUG OR SUBSTANCE ABUSE

Substance or drug abuse is a common youth problem. There are eight facts to keep in mind when considering teen substance abuse:

1. Alcohol is the most commonly abused substance.
2. Cigarette smoking is a leading cause of death in the United States.
3. Nicotine is the most addictive substance.
4. There are different types of drug use. Some are more dangerous than others.
5. Cocaine and other drugs are distributed to elementary-school-age children in almost all parts of the country and in all socioeconomic groups.
6. The best insurance against drug abuse is a loving and open relationship between parent and child.
7. Parents need to know how to talk to their children about substance experimentation, use, and abuse.
8. Parents need to be aware of the signs of drug abuse, while understanding that other problems may mimic drug abuse.

Now let's fill in some information for issues related to the above list.

TYPES OF DRUG ABUSE

It's important to understand that there are many types of drug use and abuse. Some are more dangerous than others. The largest group of drug abusers is adults. The legal substances of nicotine and alcohol kill more Americans, by far, than illegal drugs. Nicotine is now thought to be the most addictive of *all* drugs, including cocaine. Awareness of these facts can help us keep things in perspective, which is often lost these days.

Drug use falls into three categories: *drug experimentation, drug use,* and *drug abuse.* Most children, unfortunately, will experiment with drugs sometime during adolescence. However, of those who experiment, most *do not* go on to use or abuse drugs—although it is also true that almost all who abuse cocaine and other dangerous drugs started out experimenting with nicotine or alcohol first. But experimentation with nicotine or alcohol does not necessarily lead to experimentation with or abuse of "harder" drugs.

HOW TO DRAW THE LINE ON DRUG USE

Parents must take a hard line around drug experimentation and abuse without becoming angry. This may be difficult, but it is essential. Parents who are willing to be consequential and not rescue their children tend to be quieter and less noisy. Anger, shouting, and ranting all decrease the teen's self-image and put stress on the parent-child relationship. When teens and parents fight, it simply makes drug use more likely.

Substance abuse does not happen in a vacuum. It is directly related to the parent-child bond of love and good communication. We can't order our teens not to take drugs. As a matter of fact, drug use is usually a sign of rebellion. Orders, therefore, are bound to make the problem worse. Instead of orders, we should offer our thoughts and opinions of drug experimentation and abuse, and then allow consequences, without jumping in to rescue our teens.

Parents have an obligation to take care of themselves and make that commitment clear to the teen. Therefore they need to let their teens know, calmly and clearly, that if illegal drugs are in the home that makes parents accessories to crime. They should communicate to their teens that if necessary, in order to protect themselves, they will call the police and grant them permission to search the premises.

Similarly, if the teen is drinking and driving, the parent will simply phone the sheriff or highway patrol, give them the license plate number of the car, and tell them that teens in the car may be risking their own and others' safety on the highway.

We should state these realities to our teens in a loving, matter-of-fact way. They need to know that we don't want to live with the guilt we would experience if they killed someone while drinking and driving, and we had suspected the problem but done nothing.

Remember, *statements about taking good care of ourselves and refusing to become accessories to crime are much more effective than lecturing teens about what's good for them.* We can let our kids know that if *we* get in trouble for drug use, we won't expect them to hire lawyers and bail us out. Likewise, we won't bail out our kids. All drug users, we can say, must deal with the law on their own.

INFORMING OUR TEENS ABOUT DRUGS

It's essential for us to obtain fact-based articles about drug abuse and suggest our children read them. If we don't *force* our teens to read information, they will generally be interested when we provide straightforward and informative evidence.

Girls particularly need to know about the effects of drugs during the first trimester of pregnancy. In Dade

County, Florida, for example, currently more than *ten thousand* infants are born each year to cocaine-addicted mothers. These children are at high risk for having learning disorders and developmental difficulties.

SIGNS OF DRUG USE

Socially, signs of drug use and abuse may include a sudden worsening of school grades or sudden changes in friendships at school. Sometimes, a drug abuser will experience mood and attitude changes for no apparent reason.

Physically, use of marijuana leads to a red-rimmed appearance of the eyes. Acute signs of drug abuse may include enlarged pupils. Kids on amphetamines may appear overly paranoid, or they seem to have a chip on their shoulder all the time. Highs may be followed by depressive lows.

There are medical problems, however, that closely parallel the symptoms of acute drug abuse. Manic depression is one example. Also, natural physiological changes associated with adolescence can trigger behavioral fluctuations. A child who has previously been doing very well in school may suddenly appear angry, accompanied by an abrupt drop in grades. This shift usually occurs around ages fourteen or fifteen, more often in girls than boys.

WHAT TO DO WHEN YOU SUSPECT DRUG USE

If you suspect drug use, here is what we suggest you do:

First, *remain calm*. Drug use is *not* an emergency. As with other crises, drug use may have been going on for a long time, but it only becomes a crisis when we find out about it.

Second, *talk it over with your teen*.

Third, *talk to the school counselor*.

Fourth, *find out if your teen's friends and siblings are*

concerned. This is not an issue of others "ratting" on your teen. True friends and family members shouldn't maintain silence if your teen is engaged in self-destructive behavior.

Confronting substance abuse provides an excellent opportunity to open lines of communication between parent and teen. But remember that if you respond by getting upset and angry over your teen's drug use, you will most likely worsen the problem.

Pearl 14

❖

EATING DISORDERS

Louise looked in the mirror for the twentieth time that day and cursed. "I can't seem to lose any weight," she sobbed softly.

Actually, Louise had lost a lot of weight in the past half year. Her clothes hung loosely around her bony figure. But it still wasn't good enough for her. She still looked fat, or so she thought.

She rarely hung around for dinner, and when she did, she just picked at her food. Afterward, she would often head directly to the bathroom, put a finger down her throat, and throw up what she had eaten only a few minutes before.

Louise's eating disorder can kill her if she doesn't get help. Approximately 10 percent of teens with anorexia die — even with treatment.

No one is really sure what causes anorexia. It may be linked to depression in the family, especially the mother's depression. Studies indicate that it occurs in one of every twenty-five thousand females. The average woman who becomes anorexic starts out weighing between 140 to 150 pounds and may drop to as little as 70 pounds, apparently unaware of the physical consequences of such drastic weight loss. But there are no "typical" cases of anorexia; they vary from person to person.

Although there are cases of boys becoming anorexic, the disease has primarily affected females. Almost always, those females are in the young reproductive phase of their lives. Anorexia usually starts when a girl feels insecure, is made fun of, or feels that her femininity is threatened. It accelerates with vomiting (bulimia), constipation, and the cessation of menstruation. The girl aggravates the problem with intense physical activity.

Some girls who turn anorexic are deluded into thinking that they can ward off pregnancy by staying thin. Other young women are fast-track professionals who believe the only way they can compete in a "man's world" is to be thin.

As the girl gets thinner, she becomes the center of attention. This traps parents who recognize their daughter has a problem but don't want to draw attention to it. Parents make her anorexia worse by encouraging her to eat more.

Because the circumstances surrounding anorexia and other eating disorders vary so much, the best recourse for parents is to seek professional help for their child. Sometimes antidepressant medications may be helpful.

Pearl 15

---❖---

FRIENDS AND PEER PRESSURE

Parents worry a lot about who their teens' friends are. In general, they worry too much.

First, your teen's choice of friends is potentially a control battle that you can't win. It's just like the unwinnable control battle parents try to fight over what kinds of clothes their teen wears.

Second, teens learn to make their own decisions about how they'll live their lives when they interact with their friends. As they make those decisions, they also learn to live with the consequences of those decisions.

Third, peer pressure is a two-way street. We know that peers pressure our teen. But we often forget that our teens can be redemptive and influence their peers.

To the chagrin of most parents, teenagers want to hang around other teens who walk on the wild side. Good teenagers often have thoughts that they'd like to be a little bit wilder, a little bit more exciting. But they also know they're not going to. So how do they live out these fantasies? They pick friends who are like that. That doesn't mean they're going to be that way. It just means they've found a substitute for being so wild and outrageous themselves.

When my (Jim's) son Charlie was in high school, I used

to say, "Charlie, with friends like yours, you get to make more decisions than anybody in the whole school."

One of his friends was a druggie; another was an alcoholic. I used to think to myself, *Boy, why does he need those kids for friends?* The only thing that saved a control battle with him was that I had had enough psychological training and enough work with teens that I was able to finally bite the bullet and say to him, "You really like those guys, don't you?"

"Yeah, they're kind of exciting," responded Charlie.

"You know, they're probably lucky to have a friend like you," I said. "My guess is that more of you rubs off on them than they rub off on you."

"Yeah, they're better when they're around me because they don't do their drugs and they don't drink."

"Charlie, I knew it would be that way, and I feel happy for those guys that they have you for a friend."

But I had my doubts. My wife, Shirley, and I would go in the other room and express our many misgivings. It was just horrible. There were times when I said, "I know I'm wrong. I know I'm wrong. I've got to stop this."

But there were other times when I'd say, "I know I'm right. I know I'm right." I didn't want to indicate to Charlie that I thought his friends would rub off on him and drag him down. And the way we say those friends will rub off on our teen is to tell him or her very simply, "You're not going to be around those kids."

There is a major exception to this guideline, however. There are times when the law steps in and says your teenager cannot be around other teens because it's a violation of his or her probation. Then it absolutely must be that way, because that's the way the real world operates. When adults commit a crime and are put on probation, the law limits most of their civil rights. And it's better for a teen to learn that early in life. If your teen is put on probation, you should be sad for him or her. "Well, I'm really sad it's happened to you. That would really be too bad if you violated your probation."

Other than this exception, we should tell our teens, "You know, you get to make a lot of tough decisions when you're with friends like those. But I guess if anybody can make those decisions, it's you, right? And not only that, but if anybody can make some bad decisions and live with the consequences, I'll bet you can do it. So best of luck around those friends."

Then, when your teen leaves the house, you can rest assured that he or she at least has this idea in mind: "I'm in charge of me, not other kids."

Pearl 16

❖

Grades

Parents are understandably concerned and frustrated when their teens have trouble motivating themselves to take school seriously or work for good grades.

There are, however, levels of concern. The more responsible the teen, the less involved the parent ought to be.

But when teens aren't responsible—constantly failing to bring books home or losing homework—and parents try to get involved in making them do homework, it becomes a control battle that only the teen can win. The parents get indignant and give lectures, which in turn play into their teens' hands. Teens love to see their parents all worked up.

Instead, it is vital that we explore the situation from teens' point of view and try to elicit their feelings in the process. The best guarantee of graduation—or, more strategically, the best route to helping our teens maintain a healthy self-image—is to keep the doors of communication open by taking interest in our teens' lives without rescuing them.

WHY TEENS LACK MOTIVATION

Each case of poor school motivation is an individual issue, so we will review only the main causes.

Teens get tired of keeping up with the demands. High school is a time of intense competition, academically and socially. Few teens are not tired of the high school routine before it is completed. The most common mistake that parents make is to try to shove children into graduation. This almost always fails. Or, when it is successful, the children often fail their first semester of college or their first job.

There comes a time when no adult can push another to success. It's often best simply to let our kids know that we hope they will graduate — but if they reach the point where school is unimportant, then they are really saying by their actions that they are ready for life and employment.

Depression or learning disorders. If parents suspect that their teens are depressed or hampered by a learning disorder, they should seek competent professional testing and counseling. Berating a student who is suffering from problems like these will only make high school under-achievement worse.

Peer pressure. When teens are running with a peer group that does not value school, it may help if we let them know that we hope some of them rubs off on their friends. We should let our teens know that we're concerned, but it hardly ever does any good to forbid them from seeing their friends.

Preoccupation with other interests. Some teens do poorly because they have a specific consuming interest in something else. Some of America's great entrepreneurs dropped out of high school to start their own businesses. This is not to say that dropping out should be encouraged — but it's not the end of the world, either. If your child maintains a good self-image, it's a good bet that later on he or she will obtain a GED or high school equivalency degree and perhaps attend college as an adult.

Substance abuse. If teens' low motivation is related to drug abuse, then the issue is drugs, not poor school achievement.

LETTING TEENS OWN THEIR GRADES

You can head off a lot of control battles at the pass by allowing your teen to own his or her own grades. As a helpful perspective, remember that a "C" is a satisfactory grade, and most of us in life get "Cs" in almost everything we do. Most of us drive "C," eat "C," and clean house "C." A little understanding about average grades can go a long way.

Teenagers must be taught to view their own success or failure in school as belonging directly to them. Many children have problems in school out of conscious or unconscious rebellion, thinking that if they fail, their parents — not they themselves — will suffer. The important issue is to maintain a good parent-child relationship through non-accusatory questions, maintaining interest without anger, and letting the consequences naturally fall.

Watch how this love-and-logic parent handles this situation.

> DAD: "Hey, Steve, how goes school these days?"
>
> STEVE: "Great. Laura and I are hitting the class party tonight."
>
> DAD: "Super! I hope you have a good time. How are the mid-quarter grades?"
>
> STEVE: "I have some English and math assignments that the teacher wouldn't even *look* at because they were a day late. School's a drag!"
>
> DAD: "That's disappointing. So what are the grades?"
>
> STEVE: "About a C, two Ds, and two Fs."
>
> DAD: "Um . . . what's your thought on that?"
>
> STEVE: "I can pull them up . . . if I try."
>
> DAD: "Trying can be hard sometimes. I was thinking you might be happier if you were out of school and it wouldn't be so much of a drag."
>
> STEVE (shocked): "You mean just *quit*?"
>
> DAD: "Well, isn't that sort of where you're at now?"

STEVE: "Yeah, but . . ."

DAD: "See, Steve, here's what I'm thinking. I love you and want to provide for you, but all the stuff you enjoy around here—the TV, the heat, all the food—is because I do an average to good job at work. Since you're not into doing an average job in school right now, I find myself becoming a little resentful, and I love you too much to let that continue. So I'm wondering if it isn't time for you to make your way in the world, or if you choose to stay here, start working and pay board and room or whatever. You know? I just don't want to have bad feelings about you."

STEVE: "Gee, Dad, I'm going to graduate—I'll work harder."

DAD: "Well, why don't we give it one last quarter, and if you get a C in school, and I'm continuing to get a C at work, we're even. But if next quarter, the grades are still low, and things are still a drag at school, I'll expect you to start a job and start paying room and board within three weeks. You're a great worker, and you'd be great at McDonalds."

STEVE: "Well, I'm not leaving here!"

DAD: "Well, good luck, son. How do you think it will work out?"

STEVE: "The math teacher said I could get the late papers in tomorrow, but I'd have to miss the party. . . ."

DAD: "That would be a bummer. Tough bind! Hope you work it out. Love ya, Steve."

Pearl 17

❖

GROUNDING

The real world doesn't "ground" people, except in jail. Expressing your concerns with your teenager works better than grounding. A lot of parents who may be grounding their teens would be surprised to find out that they don't have to do it at all. Discipline works just as well without it.

In fact, grounding teenagers is about as silly as trying to ground a spouse.

I (Foster) often think how I would feel about it if it happened to me. Say I'm driving home a little too fast and the police pull me over and give me a ticket. I arrive home upset and tell my wife, "Gee, I was doing seventy under the bridge on I-70, and I got a ticket."

"What!" she yells. "Well, you thought we were going skiing next weekend, didn't you, Foster? But we're not. You're grounded!"

Can you imagine the irritation I would feel?

Of course, if you've tried all other methods for discipline and grounding works, then by all means give it a shot. But do it reluctantly, because your teen's future spouse isn't going to be able to use it on him or her. The only way the real world grounds us is when the police throw us in a cell. So use grounding with great care.

I (Jim) didn't ground any of my children. I found that talking over a problem and letting them live with the consequences of their decisions worked much better.

I've noticed that the people who seem to use grounding most effectively are parents who already have a really good relationship with their kids. Their teens will do almost anything for them, so the kids will put up with the grounding. The parents who can never make it work are usually struggling with poor relationships with their teens and are hoping to overpower their youngsters.

I suggest that grounding should be used on a once per child per lifetime basis. Save it for the worst thing your teen is ever going to do. It very quickly loses its effectiveness after the first time.

Pearl 18

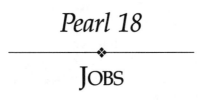

JOBS

Until recently, working at a part-time job was a sign of teenage maturity. Teens learned responsibility and time management, and they made some money for college or vocational training on top of it all.

Those motives for holding down a part-time job have changed, however. Studies have shown that many teens work not to save money for the future, but to maintain a materialistic lifestyle of consumption. They often spend their money on clothes, music, food, and other items that are discarded in a few months.

What should parents do when their teen wants to get a part-time job? Wise parents know they can't control whether their teen works outside the home, just like they can't control who the teen's friends are. However, they *can* control their own expectations of their teen. Those expectations, as we have outlined previously, are: maintain a C average or above at school, do the household chores, and respect Mom and Dad.

Here's a scenario of how a love-and-logic mom deals with her daughter and her excitement over a job.

KATHY: "Hey, Mom, I got the job at the restaurant. The boss wants me to start this Saturday."

MOM: "That's great, Kathy. How many hours a week are you going to work?"

KATHY: "The boss said fifteen, but if I do a good job he'll increase them to twenty."

MOM: "I'm glad he believes in you. But how are you planning to maintain your grades and do your chores around the house? You got a D in math last term, and I've had to lean on you as it is to do the dishes after dinner. Besides, what do you plan to do with the money you'll earn?"

KATHY (whining): "Aw, Mom. Aren't you proud of me that I'm working?"

MOM: "Answer my questions, please."

KATHY: "Well, my clothes are so *old*, and I need to buy those new albums that just came out."

MOM: "Are you planning on saving any of that money for college?"

KATHY: "Well, I don't know. You're paying for college, aren't you?"

MOM: "Well, I don't know, either, Kathy. We agreed that we'd pay for your tuition and other expenses at the state university. But you'll need to raise your grades if you have any hope of even getting accepted. If you don't get in, our paying for college is a dead issue, isn't it? And if you keep slacking off in doing your chores, we may have to come to some sort of agreement about your paying for room and board."

KATHY: "Gee, Mom, you make it all sound so harsh."

MOM: "Well, Kathy, that's how the real working world is. You see, Dad and I work because it's financially better for us to do that than it is to stay home. But working to get ahead involves sacrificing some things, such as buying the latest clothes or cars. And it also means that we all need to pay the bills and do our chores."

KATHY (crestfallen): "Well, if you don't want me to have the job, I'll call the boss and tell him I can't work."

MOM: "I'm not saying you can't have the job, Kathy. But I am asking you how you plan to balance the responsibilities of your job with your responsibilities at home."

KATHY: "Well, I can ask the boss to give me only one shift one day a week. I think I can arrange my time better to get my schoolwork and chores done. Is that okay, Mom?"

MOM: "That sounds fine to me. But if your grades drop any further in the next six weeks, what do you think should happen with the job?"

KATHY: "I guess I'd have to quit."

Part-time employment by teens can still be a good experience for them. Many teens learn valuable lessons about life and responsibility by working, not to mention reaping the monetary rewards of their labors. But parents and teens need to keep the lines of communication open so the responsibility of a job doesn't become an arena of conflict.

Pearl 19

❖

MOOD SWINGS

Remember the central figure in Robert Louis Stevenson's story *The Strange Case of Dr. Jekyll and Mr. Hyde*? Dr. Jekyll discovered drugs that transformed him into a vicious, brutal creature named Mr. Hyde. As the effects wore off, he reverted back to the kindly Jekyll.

Sometimes our teens seem like modern versions of Jekyll and Hyde. When they're in a particularly bad mood, we may wonder if they're on drugs or are facing some other awful crisis.

If your teen's mood swings are making you dizzy, keep these helpful hints in mind:

Mood swings are typical in adolescence. During the period of about five years when teens are hurtling through the physical changes that transition them from childhood to adulthood, Jekyll-and-Hyde behavior comes with the territory. The intense physical and emotional changes of adolescence are usually responsible for drastic mood swings.

Don't interrogate your teen. The worst thing we can do to depressed teens is fire questions at them: "What's the matter with you?" or "Why don't you snap out of it?" To them, that's like putting them on the witness stand while the prosecutor launches a courtroom attack!

Instead, we should acknowledge what we see and let our teen know we're available to talk. We can try caring words such as, "I wonder if you're hurting right now?" Then wait to hear what our teen says. If our teen doesn't want to talk, it's time for us to back off.

Encourage your teen to share feelings. It's okay to ask your teen, "Are you mad at me right now?" or "Have I done something to hurt you?" It will help both of you if your teen shares his or her feelings with you.

One father learned a valuable but difficult lesson from his son Jeremy. Ron and his wife sought counseling for Jeremy because he was depressed for a long time. It took many sessions with a therapist to coax Jeremy into talking about what was going on inside him.

It turned out that Jeremy thought his dad was mad at him all the time. Jeremy finally asked Ron, "Are you mad at me today?" Surprised, Ron answered, "No." Jeremy then asked, "Then why are you frowning at me?" Ron answered that he frowns when he thinks hard. He learned from his son that it makes others think he is angry. Ron had thought he had a great relationship with Jeremy, while for years Jeremy suffered under the impression that his father was always angry at him.

Most bad moods don't require a counselor. Unless your teen's depression continues over a long period for no apparent reason, there is usually no reason to seek professional counseling. Your teen's bad moods may have nothing to do with you. If you have approached your teen about the sadness or depression, and it lasts no more than about two weeks, it's usually better to let the matter rest.

Pearl 20

❖

MUSIC

Don't criticize. It will not make you a more effective parent.

Tell yourself, "There are four things I absolutely must not criticize: my teen's clothes, hair, friends, and music."

And this means we shouldn't try to slide our opinions in under cover by criticizing the clothes, hair, friends, or music of our teens' peers. Despite our occasional feelings to the contrary, our teens weren't born yesterday! They'll immediately know that we're really criticizing them.

Quarrels over music, like quarrels over television, may be more destructive to relationships and the ability to show love than the actual content of the music or TV show merits. It is very easy for parents to become destructive about things they believe might be destructive!

Parents can avoid a lot of arguments simply by accepting these facts: (1) to most teens, music is very important, and (2) most adolescents go through a phase in which they like the beat and the volume. It's hard for most of us to realize how much teens want to feel that their opinions are respected.

Since the fifties, music has been so intertwined with teen culture that it's impossible to separate the two. You can get great insights into your teen's way of thinking and relating to others by understanding his or her music. It wouldn't take that much effort for you to become conversant about musicians and bands by reading the paper and watching television. If you feel really daring, ask their permission to listen to their albums.

Although pop music trends change rapidly, the central role of music in our culture tends to remain steady. Many of the popular musicians from our teen years have found new audiences today. Even the "big band" sounds from our parents' generation have found new life among some teens. The best way to get your teen to accept and enjoy other kinds of music is for you to enjoy listening to other kinds of music and talk about why you like them.

How should we respond to our teen's music preferences? Blanket approval from a distance is certainly naive, because much of today's popular music is saturated with violent or sexually explicit themes.

However, blanket condemnation is not the answer, either. Even bands notorious for their immoral lifestyles have created beautiful love songs and insightful social commentary. Teens no more appreciate parents roundly castigating their music and its creators as immoral than parents like teens knocking all business as corrupt.

Some of us find it awkward to talk with our teens about their music. We can ease the awkwardness by asking them questions instead of just telling them what we think. If they don't want to talk about the subject, it's best to politely drop the conversation. Our graciousness at this point may come back in a blessing later on when they feel free to talk to us about their music.

If your teen pumps up the volume so loud that it disturbs you or other family members, make a deal like this one: "Hey, you're free to listen to your music, and we're free to listen to our music. Neither one of us pushes our music on the other. Try to keep it down — or could you try wearing headphones?"

This approach will get the best results. If we just criticize our teen's preferences, we might pay dearly later on when the damage of the criticism outweighs the effects of those often temporary listening habits.

Pearl 21

❖

ORDERS:
TO GIVE OR NOT TO GIVE

Ordering a teenager to do something (or not do something) is essentially an irrevocable act. Once you've handed down that order, you've burned a bridge behind you. If you change your mind, you can't cross back to where you were, because recalling an order breeds disrespect.

Another liability in giving orders is that it tends to lower teens' self-image. Maybe this is why most of us don't like taking orders! The armed services have to *train* people to be good order-takers. Telling a person what to do covertly says, "Even if you had adequate information, you could not figure out the situation for yourself."

Of course, giving orders is sometimes justified in emergency situations where, correctly, one person must say to another, "There isn't time to give you the facts of the situation now, so just do it my way!"

Giving orders works only when there is agreement on two points:

1. *Order-givers must be in unquestioned authority.* The army works very hard to make sure that troops do not question the authority figure. But teens thrive on questioning authority figures.

2. *Order-takers must accept the idea that they could not make*

a wise decision on their own. The army works very hard at this. When I (Foster) went into basic training, our training sergeant immediately told us, "Okay, you mens, you is not here to think. You is here to do. *I* is here to think. I says and you does. Do you get the picture?" But teenagers tend to think they know everything!

It's evident that when loving parents share their concerns and thoughts, children learn to respect and consider their opinions — especially when parents are right! Of course, when parents are not right, and express concerns and thoughts about issues that never even occur, teens rightly learn that their parents' thoughts and opinions are sometimes fallible. That, of course, is good thinking, too: either way, the teen learns.

WHY WE SHOULD HARDLY EVER GIVE ORDERS

So when should we give orders? Ideally, *only on rare occasions.* Usually, we should be giving our children covert messages that they will respect our ideas and our thoughts and will be able to figure out answers for themselves. However, when our kids are in danger, it's reasonable for us to say, "You can't do that."

This brings us to a second important guideline for giving orders: We should give orders *only if we can reasonably expect our child to obey, and only if we're able to apply meaningful consequences to disobedience.* By definition, once an order is given it has to be followed "or else."

The next question, of course, is *or else what?* This "or else" is very important. Every week in psychotherapy I (Foster) deal with very unhappy parents who have no "or else." They have given their child an order that the child will not obey. They often cannot even check whether it is obeyed. Then on top of that, they can't effectively apply consequences to the misbehavior! Remember: Never give an order until you have first thought of a consequence if

your teen fails to comply. Such orders include:
"Turn in *all* your homework."
"Don't smoke when you're away from home."
"Don't hang out with those friends."
"Don't drink at the party."
"Don't try drugs."
"Behave yourself, the way we taught you."

Good luck on the above list! We grownups sometimes have trouble making ourselves behave—let alone making our teenagers do what we told them!

Here are a few examples of orders given with consequences that are available to most parents to apply to disobedience:

"Don't smoke in the house (or else I'll ask you to step outside)."

"Don't have drugs in your room (or else I'll call the police)."

"Don't be disrespectful to me (or else I'll ask you to leave)."

ALTERNATIVES TO GIVING ORDERS

What's our alternative to giving orders? We'll put ourselves in the best position by *sharing our own concerns and thoughts, because that's what we have control over.*

In place of orders, thoughtful parents might say phrases like these:
"I would appreciate it if. . . ."
"I would really like you to. . . ."
"I'm hoping that. . . ."

With this approach, it's not such a big deal when our teen disregards our thoughts, opinions, wishes, and hopes. We can handle that, and it does not increase our child's disrespect. As we pointed out, if a teen directly disobeys an order and we can't thoughtfully apply consequences to the disobedience, our child will lose respect for us. This occurs because *every parent is a part of the child's own self-image: a disobedient child loses self-respect.*

Most parents tend to give orders to their teens around "very important" issues. But it's not the "importance" of the issue that matters; it's these variables:

1. Will teens obey the order?
2. If not, will we know if they have disobeyed?
3. If they have disobeyed, can we effectively apply consequences to the disobedience?

Pearl 22

❖

PARTIES

Many teens dream about the fun parties they'll attend or host when their parents are away. And while they dream, their parents try to think of ways to restrict their party activities—often with unsuccessful results. The following guidelines can be helpful to parents faced with these kinds of situations.

Never give an order you can't enforce. Parents' orders often backfire. This is because the teens who need orders also disobey them, while those who follow them probably don't need them!

It's far more effective to say, "I don't want you to host a party while we're away," or "I'm hoping you'll avoid parties where drugs are present." Then, if your teen disobeys your expectations, you have not lost as much as if your teen disobeys a direct order.

Wise parents get serious, not angry, about party behavior. They get serious by letting consequences unfold.

When John's parents were out of town, he threw a party that resulted in damage to the family's new stereo system. In a calm manner, John's father let him know that repairs were totally his responsibility. After several time-consuming trips to the repair shop and a $370 bill, John appeared less interested in being a host. "Parties can be real expensive," he said.

Wise parents keep lines of communication open without rescuing. They listen (even to information they don't want to hear), remain loving, and never confuse *acceptance* of party behavior with *approval.*

Prohibit attendance at parties only when a teen will obey the order and truly can't cope with the setting. Make sure both criterion of this rule are met before prohibiting your teen from going to a party.

For example, Paul attended a party where alcohol was served, despite his father's warning. His father had decided that no matter what happened, Paul would be able to cope. Later, after breaking up the party, police contacted Paul's father and asked him to pick up his son. Despite accusations of negligence, he refused.

Instead, Paul spent the night in detention learning some valuable lessons. "I should have listened to my dad," he said, adding, "I can handle detention once, but never again!"

Require your teen to tell you where he or she is and when he or she will return. Why should teens let us know where they are going and when they will return? Most parents answer, "Because we worry!" But that response usually leads to even less responsible behavior by teens. Love-and-logic parents *do* need to know their teens' whereabouts—because they promise *not* to worry!

An effective thing to say is, "As long as we know where you are and when you'll return, we promise not to worry. It is only when we don't know that we find ourselves worrying. We appreciate your help on this."

Pearl 23

❖

PROFESSIONAL HELP: WHEN TO SEEK IT

A delicate question often comes up for parents of troubled teenagers: "When should we decide to seek professional help?"

Seeking professional help is not an admission of failure. In our complex society, with its countless social problems, our teens quite naturally face dilemmas that we never had to cope with during our childhood.

For example, overwhelming societal pressures for success are filtering down even to the lower grades. Peer pressure prompts *kindergartners* to insist on Calvin Klein jeans and Air Jordan sneakers. More children than ever before are having severe problems, and the causes of those problems stand apart from the method or intent of parental discipline.

There are two basic reasons for considering the option of professional help:

1. *A steadily deteriorating situation for at least a three-month period with no improvement in sight.* In this case, professional help may be necessary to reverse the downward trend.

2. *Abrupt, dramatic changes in mood or behavior.* If your basically responsible and responsive teen suddenly changes his or her overall demeanor (grades go down dramatically,

friendships drop off), you may want to seek professional help immediately.

Don't assume that professional care has to involve a long, drawn-out series of counseling sessions. One session with a trained and competent counselor may be enough to straighten out the problem.

Here are some guidelines for finding the right professional care:

1. Find a therapist who has a busy schedule. A busy professional with many clients is most likely on the right track.
2. Seek out satisfied clients. Ask the therapist to give you a list of a few satisfied clients you can talk with.
3. A good therapist should be willing to give you a free half-hour session to discuss your situation.
4. Look at what's going on in the professional's life. Does this person have a good marriage? Are the counselor's children well-adjusted?
5. Get professional recommendations. Talk with pediatricians, school counselors, and psychiatric or pediatric nurses. Pick the person whose name comes up three times. If hospitalization is recommended, make sure the person recommending it is working outside that hospital system.

Pearl 24

❖

RUNAWAYS

Parents are rightly terrified when their children run away from home. But they can turn such an incident into a significant learning opportunity.

Take the case I (Foster) had with two adolescent girls, Debbie and Connie. Both had overprotective parents. Both got tired of it and ran away together one summer to Vancouver, British Columbia—which is a very pretty city, especially during the summer.

The parents came into my office. They were angry and upset about their children running away from home. I offered some advice. One set of parents listened. One set of parents didn't.

Summer drifted into fall, then winter. It was getting cold in Vancouver.

DEBBIE'S PARENTS GOT ANGRY

When Debbie phoned home, her parents started getting angry. They wanted to punish their daughter, but they wouldn't allow the consequences of her actions to take place. They demanded to know where she was.

"Vancouver," Debbie told them.

"Well, that really makes us mad!" They blew up on the phone. "You should have been phoning us! We haven't heard from you! Who do you think we are? You get home right now!"

"I don't have any money," complained Debbie.

"Well, we'll send you money to get home, but when you get home—we're telling you right now—you're going to be grounded for three months! Do you understand?"

"Yes," said Debbie.

"All right! You stay right there; we'll send you the money."

Debbie's parents sent her the money with the warning that she would be grounded when she got home. Debbie came home for about two weeks, and then she ran away again.

CONNIE'S PARENTS STAYED CALM

When Connie phoned home, her mom and dad showed no anger. Rebellious teens love anger, but there wasn't any to react to.

"Well hi, honey!" they low-keyed it. "Where have you been?"

"Vancouver," answered Connie.

"Well that's a nice city. You been having fun up there?"

"Oh, yeah."

"What have you been doing?" they inquired politely.

"Waiting tables and bumming around," Connie filled in.

"That's good! When do you think you're coming home?"

"Now?" asked Connie.

Then Mom said, "Well, that would be wonderful! We'd be glad to see you again! Let us know when you're coming in, and we'll be there."

"How will I get home?" Connie pressed.

"Well, honey, how did you there?"

"I thumbed it," Connie replied, waiting for her mother to gasp in horror and rush in to rescue her from doing it again.

(Connie's mom knew Connie was going to say that, because we had already rehearsed this conversation in my office. You know what rebellious teens are going to say long before they say it. They're often not very creative.)

"Well, Connie, how do you plan to get home?" her mom said.

"I don't know," came a little tremulous voice.

"Is there something we can do?"

"I'd like you to help."

"Hmm, Connie," Mom answered. "I've always felt that if you got yourself somewhere you should get yourself back. However, I would be willing to send you half the fare for a bus trip home if you found out how much it would cost and how we could mail the money to the bus company. Of course, you'd have to pay us back with interest after you returned home and got a job here."

A moment of silence.

Then Connie said, "Okay — I'll find a job, and then I'll come home on the bus."

"Hey, good thinking!" Connie's dad chimed in. "It probably beats thumbing home in the winter. It's cold! And of course, it's better than taking the risks of getting beat up or raped."

"Debbie's already gone because her parents paid airfare for her return," Connie said, with some resentment.

"I know, dear," Mom said. "That probably was convenient. But this is what we are willing to do, and we'd love to see you. You got yourself there by thumbing. The bus trip probably should be better than that, right?"

Acquiescing, "I guess you're right."

See how these parents are handling it? No anger, no punishment, just pure questions and consequences.

WHAT'S HARDER AT FIRST IS EASIER LATER ON

Both girls eventually pulled their lives together and became responsible adults, but Connie did it sooner. And unlike Debbie, Connie never ran away again.

We realize that the approach used by Connie's parents may seem harsh. We believe, though, that teens are tougher and more resilient than we give them credit for. As a parent, you must take the long view on what is best for your teen. If your goal is to help your teen become a responsible, productive, self-sufficient adult, you may have to take some difficult steps along the way. But what's harder at first is easier later on—for you *and* your teen.

Pearl 25

❖

SATANISM AND RELIGIOUS CULTS

Black clothes, jewelry with inverted pentacles, black candles, books describing satanic rituals – all of these can suggest involvement in satanic activity. Of all the kinds of trouble that teens can get into, and of all the ways that they may express rebellion, probably nothing frightens parents more than when their children flirt with satanism or join religious cults.

Parental attitudes of fright and overreaction make it more likely to be a problem. In many cases we're dealing with a lot of hype. We're not saying satanic activity doesn't occur or can't involve long-term emotional and spiritual damage. But it also involves hype.

Let's say police find two teens who have disemboweled squirrels. Given a choice between, "Here are two psychopathic kids cutting open squirrels" or "Here are two kids in a cult," it's easier for society to say, "We've got a cult" instead of "We've got a lot of disturbed people." We look for simplistic answers.

There is a regrettable outlook in a lot of Christian literature that satanism and religious sects are everywhere. It's our opinion, based on what the Bible says, that *God* is everywhere.

231

WHY CHRISTIAN FAMILIES ARE
ESPECIALLY AT RISK

Christian parents, especially, are at risk for two reasons on this issue.

First, *satanic activity is the Achilles heel for Christian families.* Christian parents are more likely to get emotionally involved about their teens flirting with satanism than anything else. When teens stray from the faith, they draw more parental emotion. Children like emotion, even if it's negative.

This apparent involvement works extra well for teens who have a poor relationship with their parents because it's such an effective way to get back at them. It's a great channel for a teen going through a bit of rebellion. As parents react more, teens go into it deeper. It becomes a vicious cycle.

Second, *some Christian families tend to be rigid about what children should and should not believe.* A satanic cult or religious sect is going to be as doctrinaire, rigid, authoritarian, and demanding as hyper-religious parents. Nothing really changes for teens in this case, because someone is still telling them what to do.

WHAT PARENTS SHOULD DO

So what can parents do? We recommend these six steps.

1. *Parents should first assess their own parenting techniques.* Children will go where they feel most loved. If they are rejected at home, they will go elsewhere — even if that "elsewhere" is a religious cult. Parents should ask themselves if they will love their children unconditionally, regardless of their religious persuasion.

Sometimes parents get upset that a sect teaches satanic rites, such as human or animal sacrifice. These parents are worried about the blood and gore of the sect. What they need to wonder is why their teen is interested in blood and gore in the first place. How did they raise their children?

2. *Parents should recognize that as distasteful or horrifying as it may appear, teen involvement in satanism or a religious sect is usually a phase, often subtly encouraged by a strict home environment.* When teens leave structured homes, they look around for a new structured environment, whether it's the military, a fraternity or sorority, or a strict religious group. Some of these strong groups can be seen as "transitional parents."

3. *Parents should get to know and understand the cult.* If the teen is being rebellious and parents invite a cult member over for lunch, it takes the fun away. Just be sure not to be judgmental around your teen and the other cult members.

Parents can do themselves a favor by understanding that not all alternative religious movements are alike. For example, satanism and witchcraft are two different religious systems. Also, such religious movements have high dropout rates. If Robert joins a new guru's movement, odds are good he will be out of it in a year.

4. *Parents can't control when their teens stop their involvement in a religious or satanic sect.* People have tried measures as extreme as kidnapping their teens out of cults and deprogramming them. Such actions are at best marginally effective, and they are often illegal.

When satanic activity violates the law, however, it puts the problem in a whole new category. Criminal behavior is criminal behavior. Parents are taxpayers and should take advantage of their police department.

5. *In those instances when the dangers are real and threatening the child, parents should consider moving their teen geographically.* If you feel that the potential damage to your teen of involvement with a satanic cult or religious sect is greater than the potential stress on your relationship caused by forcing your teen to move away, then you should move your teen. The home of a close family member or a reputable psychiatric hospital are possible alternatives to the present living situation.

6. *Parents need to accept it on faith that God is with their teen.* After examining their past and present parenting and making adjustments — if any — they should also have faith in their parenting. And they should have faith that their teens will ultimately make the right decisions about what to believe.

Pearl 26

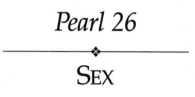

SEX

Teenage sexual activity is increasing. Recent studies indicate that a high number of girls and boys have been sexually active prior to graduation from high school. Many children, unfortunately, are sexually active in junior high school.

Parental prohibitions will not stop sex. Sex is addictive. Even a religious upbringing does not seem to correlate with whether or not teens decide to become sexually active.

I (Foster) am reminded of the father who was concerned that his daughter was sexually active. Therefore, he personally dropped her off at school in the morning and picked her up in the afternoon. What he hadn't planned on was his daughter's ingenuity. She found an opportunity and became pregnant over the noon hour.

An aggravating factor is the hypocrisy of many parents, who worry about their teen's sexual involvement while failing to handle their own sexual life in an ethical and open manner.

What's most important, fundamentally, is keeping open lines of communication between parents and teens. This communication should include the parents expressing their religious and moral values on the topic in a clear, sensitive, and straightforward fashion.

If we raise children who are honest with us about their hopes, aspirations, dreams, and sexuality, we are in pretty good shape as parents.

However, if we are open about sex, we may get questions we have a hard time answering. For example, I've heard of teens asking, "How old do I have to be to have sex?" or "When did you first have sex?" or as one thirteen-year-old asked her mom at dinner, "Mom, do you have oral sex?" The mom nearly choked to death on her chicken!

When parents are asked questions about their own sexuality—which happens when sexual matters are handled openly in the family—we suggest this rule: *Answer your children in general terms and keep your own specifics to yourself, simply reserving the right to your own privacy.*

Often, when kids ask why they should not have sex, some parents don't know what to say except *don't*. This is usually not very helpful. It's better to say something like, "Honey, I want you to really enjoy and love sex for all of your life. If you have sexual experiences that you feel bad or guilty about, it could affect the joy you have later with your spouse. Besides that, many serious diseases—like AIDS—are passed person to person through sex. For centuries many wise books, like the Bible, and various teachers have taught that sex is best saved for one person in marriage. That's why I want you to wait until you meet the person who you feel really good about. But if you ever choose to make a different choice about having sex, I hope the two of you will talk it over first, make a careful decision, and see a physician about contraception."

Because we frankly give our teens facts and thoughts on how to handle their sexual urges does not mean we are implicitly approving of premarital or promiscuous sex. Adolescent sexuality is not an issue by itself, but takes place within a loving or conflicted parent/child relationship. That relationship—in the parent's love shown to the child and in open dialogue—is the most important aspect of adolescent sexuality. Adolescent sexuality is an area in which "Just say no" will not work!

Some parents worry that talking to their child about contraception will send the wrong message that it's okay to have sex and that the parent approves. We don't believe this is the case. Teens are only a few months or years away from a plunge into adult life. They deserve our best shot at "real world" communication. In that communication we do have every right to share—not *preach*—our values. By having straightforward, honest discussions, we are sending the message "I believe you are old enough to think wisely and make responsible choices."

Children also need facts on venereal diseases, AIDS, and the risk of pregnancy. These should be presented in a cool, loving, matter-of-fact manner. When parents are unsure of facts, they can easily obtain articles and books available for teens concerning the risks of premarital sex.

Parents can talk to a child of the opposite sex about sexual issues, as long as they are not asking for details or satisfying sexual needs of their own through the child. Let's listen as a loving father talks to a responsible teenage daughter about sexual issues. The secret is to remain loving, accepting, and non-accusatory:

> DAD: "It looks like you and Greg have been dating awhile and are really happy together."
> CINDY: "We are."
> DAD: "I'm not prying at all, but I'm wondering how you and Greg are going to handle intimacy and sex."
> CINDY: "I don't know."
> DAD: "Hmm, is it something you've discussed?"
> CINDY: "Some."
> DAD: "Well, I think if you and Greg do love each other, the subject will come up. I'm hoping you talk about what it means long term, rather than have something

just happen—if you know what I mean."

CINDY: "Oh, Dad. . . . Actually, we have discussed it some. I think he's pretty interested in sex. But I just don't know."

DAD: "You know what my values are on premarital sex—we've talked about them before."

CINDY: "Yeah, Dad! I appreciate your ideas. I'm just not sure yet what I think."

DAD: "So, what if you did have sex—would you plan for it, or do you think it would just happen?"

CINDY: "I'd want to plan for it."

DAD: "Well, that's good thinking. What's your thought on having a baby?"

CINDY: "I don't want a baby yet."

DAD: "Great. Well, if I can be of help in your thinking things through, would you talk to me about it or probably not?"

CINDY: "I'd talk to you."

DAD: "Super. That makes me feel good. I know you'll consider these things carefully and make a good decision. I love you, honey."

CINDY: "I love you too, Dad."

Many parents might think that such a conversation would only encourage premarital sex. It's true that there's no guarantee what choice Cindy will make. However, she now knows that her father is not ignorant and condemning. Chances are good that she will consider her dad "safe" and a source of wisdom. The more they talk in a similar manner, the more opportunity he will have to make an impact on her behavior. If they don't talk, Dad's probably out of Cindy's decision-making loop.

We can keep the lines of communication open by being non-judgmental, non-accusatory, providing facts about the values, joys, and dangers of sexual behavior, and modeling a healthy approach to sexuality ourselves.

Pearl 27

❖

THE SILENT TREATMENT

If you're worried because your teen won't talk, don't worry! There's probably more reason to be concerned about a teen who shares everything with you. But many parents, accustomed to talkative youngsters, blame themselves when their children grow up and clam up.

It is absolutely normal for young people to withhold information from adults. Here's why:

Teens don't feel safe sharing certain things with their parents. Teens may not share embarrassing thoughts or problems with us because they think (often correctly) we won't be able to handle what they say. We have a natural tendency to become angry and upset when our teens tell us certain things. For example, it's a rare and wise parent who says when a teen admits lying to a teacher, "That's sad. I'm glad you shared that with me. How can I help you?"

Teens are seeking independence. A teen's thinking goes something like this: "If I tell my parents everything, that means I am not independent."

Teens sometimes lack the right words. Some adolescents don't talk because it may be difficult to find the words that match their feelings.

Teens are going through more changes than at any other time in life. The physical, emotional, and chemical changes taking place in a teen's body are intense. It's understandable why an adolescent behaves differently than the child who told you everything.

Teens often think they're the only ones who have certain thoughts. Intense physiological changes can make adolescents feel strange and confused. They may withdraw in the anxious feeling that "something must be wrong with me."

A few rules for parents can go a long way in encouraging teens to open up:

Don't interrogate. Parents who get the best results don't fire a lot of questions at their teenagers. Instead they say, "Let me tell you about my day!" Sometimes, their own enthusiasm rubs off.

Make it safe for your teen to talk. This means don't criticize. Don't tell your daughter she's wrong — even when she is! A teen who is criticized will talk back or clam up even more. We need to show our teens we can handle what they say without anger.

Don't try to force your teen to talk. It's a natural tendency to keep quiet when someone tries to make us talk. Withholding information also makes some teens feel they are in control. Their silent message is, "You can't make me talk!" Keep in mind that teens will talk when they're ready and only when it's safe.

It's normal and natural for teens to keep some information from adults. We're probably better off not knowing everything about them anyway!

Pearl 28

❖

SOCIAL AND EXTRACURRICULAR ACTIVITIES

Parents and teens often find themselves in the heat of battle over social and extracurricular activities. Parents legitimately expect their teens to maintain at least average grades at school. Teens argue that recreational activities can provide a way for them to socialize with their friends.

Many battles flare up from parents' belief that certain activities are just not acceptable. But here is another area in which we often confuse acceptance with approval. We forget that there is a big difference between the two.

Wise parents are more concerned about their teen's plans for handling undesirable activities than they are about restricting the activities themselves. Whether a social activity is good or bad is not nearly as important as knowing your teen can handle any temptations associated with the event. The following scenario illustrates a love-and-logic approach:

CHERYL: "Mom, I'm old enough to go to that concert. Can I go?"

MOM: "I'll know you're old enough when you can tell me about the possible pressures you're going to face and your plans for handling them."

CHERYL: "Gee, Mom. Are you worried I'll do drugs?

You know I don't do drugs."

MOM: "That's not what I said, Cheryl. I want to know what you're going to say when the other kids are telling you that everybody does drugs at a concert and that you're not going to get hooked if you do some once in a while."

CHERYL: "Gee, Mom. Don't you trust me?"

MOM: "That's not the point. I know how hard it is to be in awkward situations. I also know that once you have thought it out and come up with a plan for handling those situations you'll be ready to take care of yourself. I'll be glad to let you go to the concert when you can describe that plan to me."

This mother knows that the day Cheryl can describe her plan for handling an activity is the day that Cheryl is ready for that activity—and also the day that her mom no longer needs to worry about it.

Many of the arguments over outside activities revolve around whether that involvement will detract from school-work. Some extracurricular engagements, such as band and theater, fill educational needs even though they aren't part of a formal curriculum. Others, such as athletics, are beneficial even though they aren't academic.

When teens know their parents are listening, they are more willing to be flexible about their participation in extra-curricular activities. Observe how this love-and-logic dad and son deal with the son's desire to run track:

GARY: "Dad, the coach thinks I can make the track team!"

DAD: "I'm happy for you, Gary. But I wonder if you'll be able to keep up with your studies. You made only a C plus average last term, and I'm wondering whether that will be enough for you to be accepted to college."

GARY: "I know, Dad. I think I can do both track and school."

DAD: "How will you manage that?"

GARY: "The coach talked over my grades with me, too. We agreed that if I can't keep my average up, I'm off the squad."

DAD: "That sounds good to me. I certainly hope you make the team, and I look forward to watching you run. But remember, as I've said before, if the grades go down, paying for college tuition is squarely in your lap."

We hope our teens will discuss with us many of the things that go on in their lives. Like adults, teens make mistakes or find themselves in difficult situations. It's helpful when they can talk with an interested, non-blaming adult about these experiences. Their willingness to talk to us is a good sign. It gives them a chance to relive, in a safe way, what happened and get their own beliefs in order. Effective parents listen without being afraid that their willingness to listen in a non-blaming way means approval.

Pearl 29

❖

SPORTS

Junior wide receiver Dwight went out long. The quarterback stepped back, saw all his receivers were covered, but took his chances anyway. He cocked his arm and fired the pass thirty yards to Dwight.

Dwight jumped, reached, and snared the football. The linebacker then snared Dwight, throwing a ham-sized forearm across Dwight's chest while he was still in mid-air. The hit sent Dwight horizontal, airborne, and down. Dwight didn't hit the frozen ground so much as the ground hit him. The shock knocked the ball from his hands and kicked the air out of his lungs.

The play was over, but the action wasn't. Dwight's mother tied the high school record for the fifty-yard dash as she bolted from the stands and ran across the field toward Dwight. As she took in the sight of her fallen son gasping for breath, she whirled around to the linebacker, pointed her leather-gloved hand in his face, and screamed, "You big jerk! Don't you ever hit my son again!"

Dwight's only real regret about the play was that the ground was too hard to dig a hole in so he could crawl down it and die.

This is NOT the way parents should encourage their

teens in sports. Dwight not only lost the ball on the play, He lost his self-esteem when his mother took matters into her own hands.

Sports offer a lot for teens. They develop bodies, which we want to encourage teens to continue developing for the rest of their lives. Sports also promote team spirit, good peer relationships, and a feeling of solidarity with the school. Perhaps most importantly, sports teach teens how to handle defeat and become "good sports."

Parents can encourage their teens' athletic development by observing a few guidelines:

Guard against parental overinvolvement. Spectators at wrestling matches often see parents yelling to their sons, "Kill him! Kill him!" The wrestler doesn't need to put a hammer lock on his opponent as much as the parents need a hammer lock on their mouths. Parental screaming at sports events tends to be counterproductive as well as silly.

When conflicts arise between teens and coaches, it's usually more helpful for parents to suggest how teens should talk to their coach, rather than for parents to talk to the coach. After all, teens don't call up their parents' boss when their parents have a dispute on the job. Teens learn best when they handle such differences by themselves.

Teens should not engage in certain sports before their bodies have developed properly. Heavy weightlifting, for example, can damage undeveloped spines and certain muscle groups.

If your teen doesn't want you to attend a meet or game, talk to your teen about how your behavior might be making him or her uncomfortable. Respect your teen's wishes—change the behavior or refrain from attending.

Let your teen's interest in sports develop naturally. Teens are most likely to do well in sports when their parents take an interest in athletics but don't force it on their kids. Those who do push their teen into sports will tend to get worked up about their teen's mistakes or judgment errors. Those who encourage their teen properly will tend to get excited about what their teen does right.

I (Foster) know a young girl who is training to be a figure skater on her way to the Olympics. She benefits greatly from her mother's encouragement. She tells me that her mom constantly encourages her to "go for it." Her mother spends hours at the rink watching her practice her form and turns, cheering her on with every new move she learns.

This mom is encouraging, not forcing, her daughter to excel. Her daughter's talent is blossoming like a flower, and that blossoming is something that her daughter owns. Her mom told me once, "If she wanted to quit, it would be her decision."

This girl also notices how other mothers try to coerce their daughters into becoming the next Katerina Witt. The other girls hate it. "I see the moms pushing their kids," she says. "They even push the kids who can't skate, and the kids just end up crying." The only things these other girls are learning is that they hate to skate — and that they aren't happy with their mothers, either.

Through sports, teens can learn valuable lessons about their own identity, independence, and skills. As in other areas of their teens' lives that concern identity and independence, parents need to give their teens the freedom in sports to try, succeed and fail, and pick themselves up to try again.

Pearl 30

❖

SUICIDE THREATS

Tragically, suicide is one of the leading causes of death among teenagers. It is a sobering problem that parents must take seriously while recognizing that some suicidal threats are manipulative in nature.

It's best not to plant the word *suicide* in a teen's mind. If you have reason to be concerned, or if your teen has indirectly referred to suicide, the thought has probably already entered his or her mind.

When you do talk to your teen about suicide, show concern and caring while remaining matter-of-fact. You can make matters worse with responses such as, "You don't mean that," or "Don't ever talk like that."

The situation is usually more dangerous if a teenager has already thought of a specific lethal method and has the means at his or her disposal. Giving away favorite objects is another serious sign.

Most authorities believe the risk is higher if depression or suicide runs in the family.

A physical injury such as a concussion, loss of limbs, blindness, or paralysis can lead to severe depression, in which suicide becomes a common thought.

Teens at greatest risk are those who usually achieve

without struggle. They often expect success to be automatic and, at times when they think they are failing, have difficulty believing that the struggle to work through it will lead to solutions.

Teens who continually struggle and never succeed are also at risk. They become hopeless and want to give up on life.

Our goal in discussing suicide with our teens should be to help them pursue other options. At the same time, we should be considering other avenues of support, such as counseling, support groups, and, if necessary, hospitalization.

Here's a conversation that models talking to teens about suicide in a loving manner:

DAD: "You seem pretty down these days, Kate."

KATE (sighs): "I don't want to talk about it. . . ."

DAD: "Sometimes it seems that things are so bad there's no way out."

KATE (softening): "Yeah."

DAD: "You've been so unhappy—I wonder if you feel life just isn't worth living."

KATE (softer): "I do, Dad. It's just that everything turns out wrong. I'd probably be better off dead."

DAD: "Are there any other solutions?"

KATE: "I probably wouldn't do it. I'm too chicken. . . ."

DAD: "When I'm feeling really down, it always helps me to talk to someone else."

KATE: "Like a shrink?"

DAD: "Maybe. The nice thing about seeing a therapist is you can always quit if things don't seem better. I know, because I've been there. I hope you'll think about finding someone to talk with."

KATE: "I will, Dad. Thanks."

During this conversation, Kate's dad never becomes defensive. Instead, he stays with her feelings and lets her know what works for him when he is down. He does not force Kate into a decision. If he did, she might say "no." If he allows her to give it some thought, she might say "yes."

Explore alternatives with your teen in a loving, calm, and receptive manner, without moralizing or downplaying the problem. But if the threats escalate or lead to an actual suicide attempt, seek professional help.

Pearl 31

❖

THE TELEPHONE

The telephone is a wonderful parenting instrument! Like all instruments, it can be used appropriately by parents to help children learn responsibility and develop a consistently cheerful demeanor. On the other hand, it may be used inappropriately and lead to family squabbles.

Family phone hassles typically begin when children are young. They see that when Mom is on the phone, they are free to run around the house, cause minor furniture damage, pollute the auditory atmosphere, and generally behave in a way that they could never get away with if she were off the phone.

This control of parents around the phone often continues when childhood years slip into adolescence. Then the parents become frustrated because the child is on the phone "too much." Parents fret because homework isn't getting done. They become frustrated when they can't get their calls because their teen is monopolizing the phone.

Sometimes affluent parents throw in the towel, pay the extra bucks, and get teens their own telephone in their own room. Most parents, of course, can't afford that solution, so they muddle through.

Whatever the hassle, the child learns from toddlerhood

through adolescence: "Around phone issues, Mom and Dad end up frustrated and I end up winning!" However, as love-and-logic principles dictate, there is no such thing as a win/lose situation between parent and child. There are only *lose/lose* situations or *win/win* situations.

Love-and-logic parents use the phone to confirm that they are in loving self-control, which in turn helps the teen learn self-control and responsibility.

With the wide and inexpensive availability of call waiting service, all parents with teenagers have access to an automatic, inexpensive, and efficient answering machine. As parents of teens know, their "teen phone answering machine" always circles around the phone!

Wise parents set guidelines like these:

PARENT: "Robert, you can use the phone as much as you want. Whenever any of us is on the line, we will answer the other line when it clicks and take telephone numbers for the other family member to call back."

(Since teens are on the phone for much longer periods than their parents, they, not parents, end up being the phone answering machine.)

ROBERT: "Okay, that sounds fair to me."

PARENT: "However, there is a difference. When telephone calls come in for you, I always take the number and tell your friends that you will call them back sometime. When a telephone call comes in for an adult who is present in the home, you tell the caller that you are on the phone right now but will get off. Then you summon the adult to the phone.

"While the adult is coming to pick up the call, within two sentences you tell your friend goodbye and you'll call him back when one of the adults finishes talking, and you hand over the phone. Is the picture clear?"

ROBERT: "Yeah, it's clear, but that's unfair! How come you get to talk to people immediately and I have to wait?"

PARENT: "Because I pay the bills. Whoever pays the telephone bill gets to use the phone immediately. It's their phone. If the rule seems unfair to you, you can pay for another line and the monthly bill, and have your own phone in your room."

(This is based on the supposition that any teen responsible enough to earn his own money and pay for his own line and monthly bill is responsible enough to have his own telephone in his own room. This supposition is almost always true.)

Most children, considering this argument, will agree that adults should have immediate access to their phone calls. In return, they get to use the phone, which is a *real* privilege.

Some teens, unfortunately, need to have the following conversation with their parents:

PARENT: "Karen, how will the rules have to change to ensure that I always get my calls if my business associates or friends try to contact me but all they ever get is a busy signal or just no answer—and I discover that this is occurring while I'm home and you're on the phone?"

KAREN: "Well, I suppose you could ban me from the telephone so that it would always ring through."

PARENT: "What a good idea! Maybe we ought to give that real thought! I appreciate the suggestion. Do you think that we will need that rule?"

KAREN (snappish): "No, I guess not."

PARENT: "Thanks, Karen, you're a jewel!"

A loving parent-child relationship, firmness, and high expectations almost always ensure that you will have a pleasant, courteous, effective, and always present "answering machine" in your teen.

Pearl 32

❖

VIDEO GAMES

Not so long ago, video games offered a feeble alternative to pinball machines. Two players using crude joysticks bounced a tiny white ball back and forth on a black ping-pong table. The action was slow, but for back then it was fun.

How things have changed. Now two, three, four, or more players can search for buried treasure or battle intergalactic aliens. With a computer monitor or television set, a few joysticks, and some hardware and software, teens can spend hours living a high-tech fantasy.

And they do. The mental intensity generated by playing video games can be a healthy way for teens to learn how to use computers. But the games also can be an unhealthy obsession.

Video games are perhaps the most popular teen preoccupation. They consume hours of time that might otherwise go into studying, chores, or activities that parents think are more important. But what parents think is important doesn't really matter when it's so much easier and a lot more fun to play video games.

Some parents would say that video games are an addiction. Their teens won't or can't stop playing. There also is some concern that obsessive playing raises stress levels.

So what do parents do?

Obviously, they can't prevent their teens from playing video games when they are over at their friends' houses or when they are at an arcade at the mall. Remember: parents can't win a battle that they can't control.

But parents still have the right to expect that their teens will get average grades and do their chores. And they also have the right to insist that their teen treat family members with courtesy and respect.

When teens play their video games, they probably use the family television or computer. Like the telephone or car, the television and computer belong to the parents and the rest of the family. If teens' use of these appliances interferes with family recreation, home maintenance, or business, parents can rightly forbid teens from playing their games.

Parents, too, must assess how they spend their own recreation time. It's hypocritical to criticize teens for spending too much time playing video games while living the life of an unrepentant couch potato glued to TV sitcoms. This hypocritical behavior is a sure way to strip teens of respect for parental authority.

Video games can be wonderful instruments for recreation, for teaching eye-hand coordination, and for developing useful skills in operating computers. But like the telephone, the instrument of video games can be abused. Open communications can ensure their responsible use.

Pearl 33

❖

VIOLENCE:
BULLIES AND GANGS

A generation ago, the most a teen had to fear at school or out on the street was being accosted by bullies. In recent years, that concern has been folded into the larger specter of violence from gangs and armed students.

The advice of a generation ago for dealing with bullies is still valid today: give them a wide berth. Bullies are bullies. They don't understand decency or reason. And because they are usually gifted with size and physical strength, they can't easily be beaten on their own turf. Wise parents will not encourage their teens to try to beat up a bully. They will, however, alert school officials to harassment by bullies and let officials know that they will not tolerate such intimidation.

The rise of gangs is a different and much more frightening matter. Drive-by shootings and other violence associated with gang and drug culture have even led to schools installing metal detectors at the doors to apprehend students carrying guns, knives, and other weapons.

Gangs offer a way for young teens to find security and a family that they may not have at home. Solidarity is reinforced through secret gestures, language, drugs, and often brutal initiation rites. The danger—regardless of the shocking and senseless violence—draws teens to a lifestyle that brings the movies and the evening news right to their doorstep.

For some young people, the attraction of gang involvement is hard to resist, especially in the idea of standing out from peers as a member of an alluring and darkly romantic group. Even a strong and stable family life with both birth parents at home is no guarantee that a young teen will steer clear of joining a gang.

With many of the issues facing teens, we can offer choices, point out the results of those choices, let teens make their own decision, and then allow teens to learn how to live with the consequences of that decision. But a decision to join a gang—right and wrong issues aside—can be fatal.

Parents who find that their teens may be pressured or attracted to join a gang will probably find that they need to remove their child from the school or community situation. This is extremely hard for both parents and teens, but gang violence makes a decision imperative.

If teens insist on joining a gang, however, families may have no other recourse than to ask them to leave home. Parents need to stress that teens are marking themselves as a target for other gangs, which unacceptably places the family in a position of risk as targets for violence. Yet at the same time, teens need to be told that their family loves them and wants them more than the gang wants them.

Many families have learned to take back their communities from gangs through political or community action and church leadership. Parents have learned to band together and become a source of strength for those teens who are trying to resist the temptation to join a gang.

INDEX

AUTHORS

Foster W. Cline, M.D., is an internationally recognized child and adult psychiatrist. He is a consultant to mental health organizations, parents' groups, and schools across North America. He specializes in working with difficult children.

Jim Fay has thirty-one years of experience as an educator and principal. He is recognized as one of America's top educational consultants and has won many awards in the education field.

LOVE AND LOGIC SEMINARS

Foster Cline, M.D., and Jim Fay present "Love and Logic" seminars for both parents and educators in many cities each year. For more information on their cassette tapes, seminars, or other helpful materials, contact:

Cline/Fay Institute, Inc.
Fay Professional Building, Suite 102
2207 Jackson Street
Golden, CO 80401
1-800-338-4065